Giovanna Sandri
CAPITOLO ZERO

DABA
New York

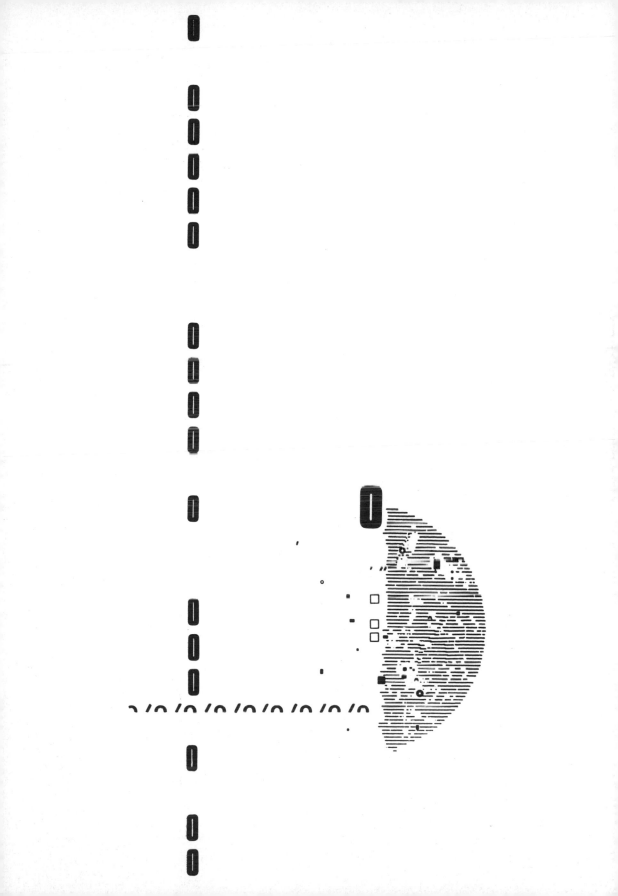

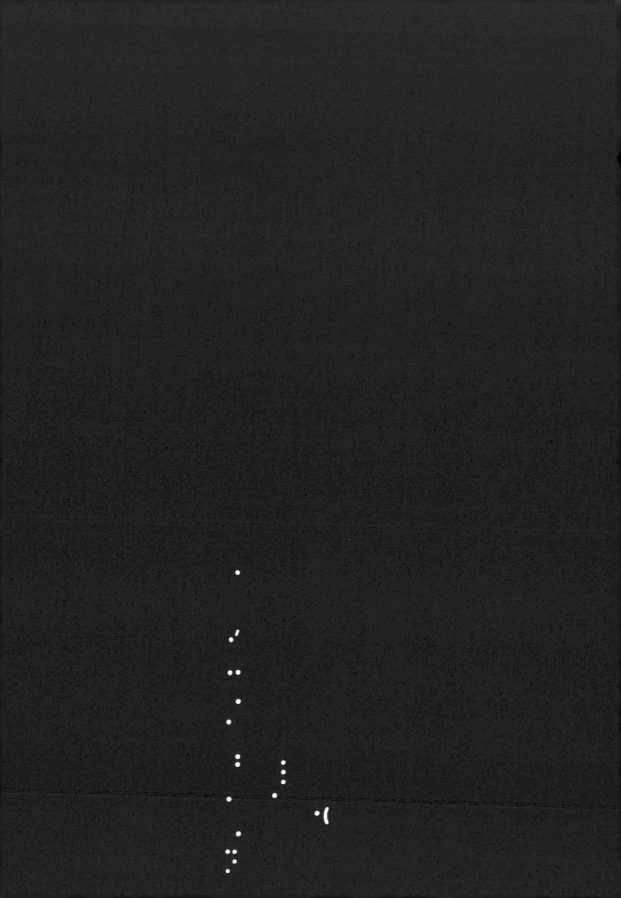

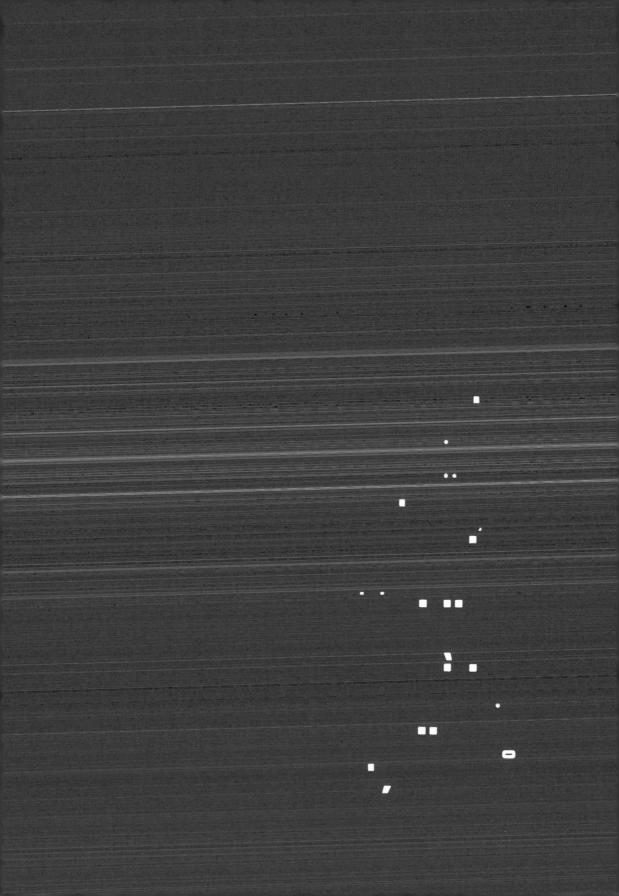

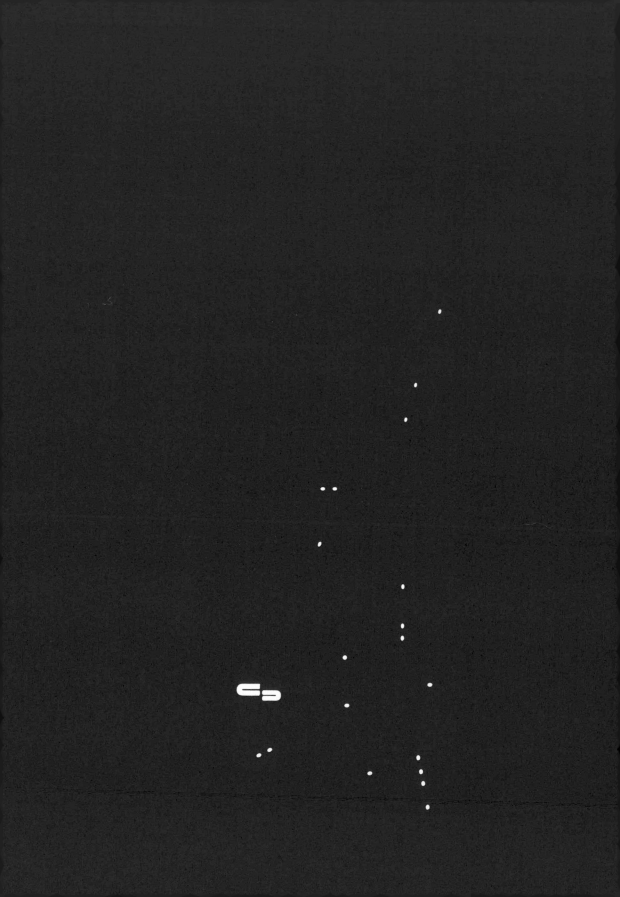

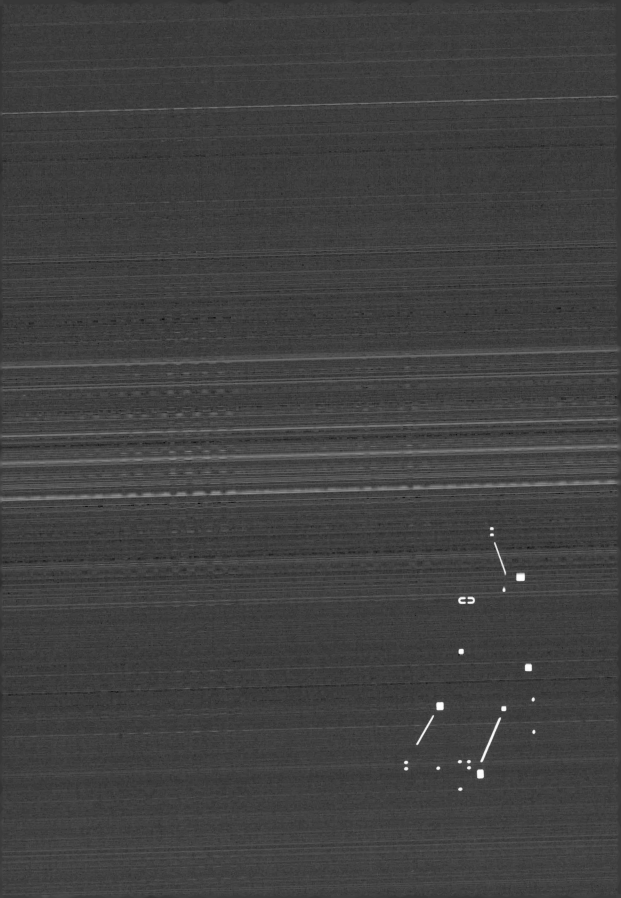

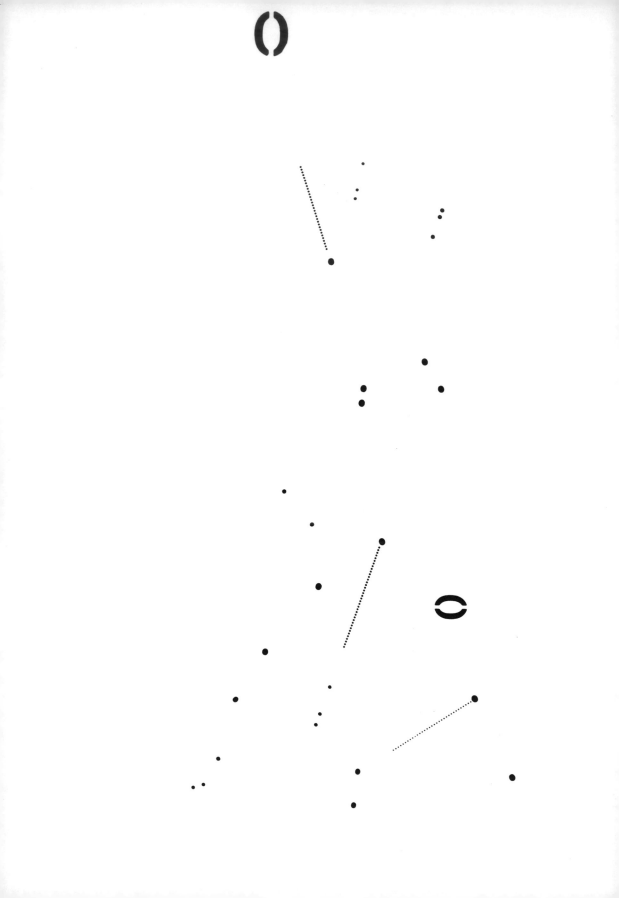

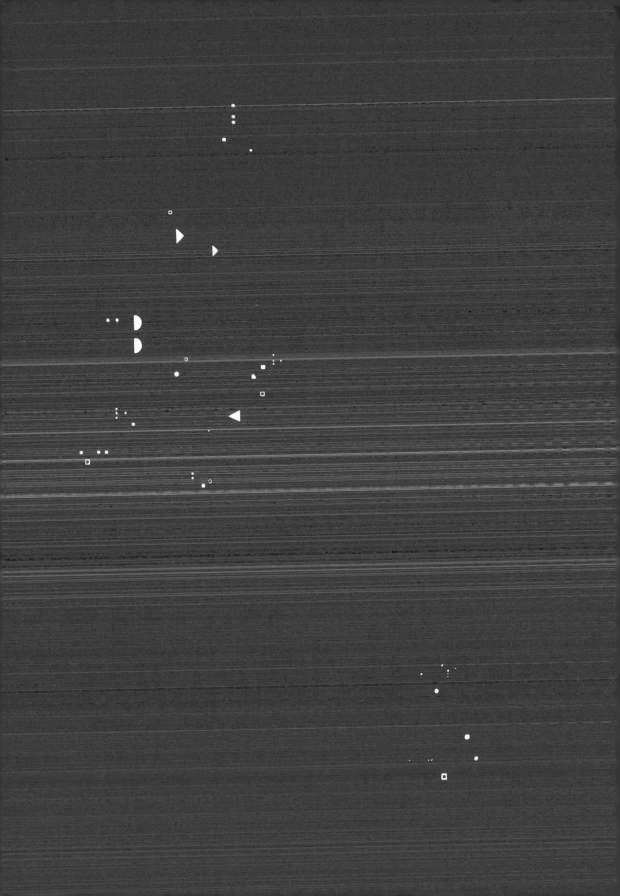

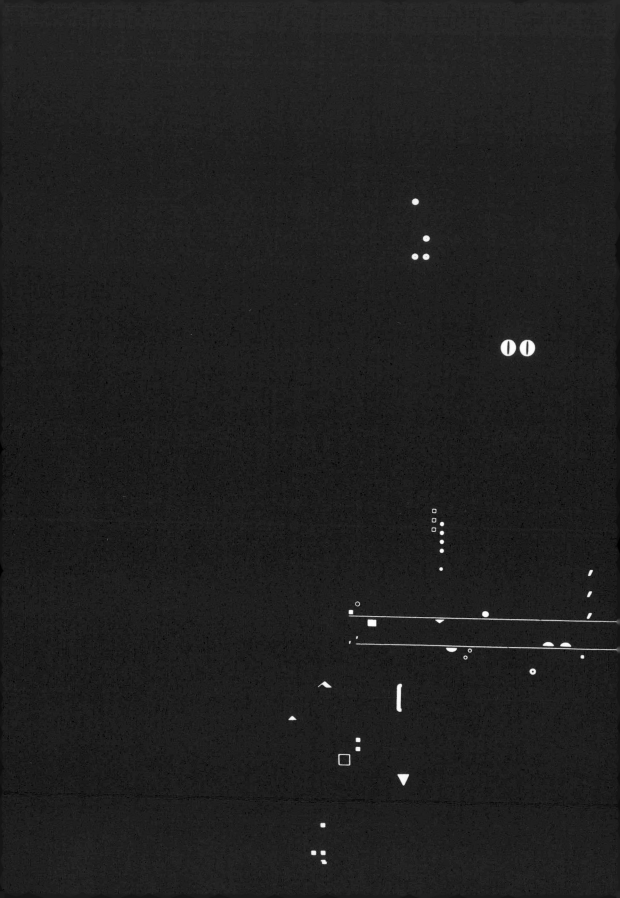

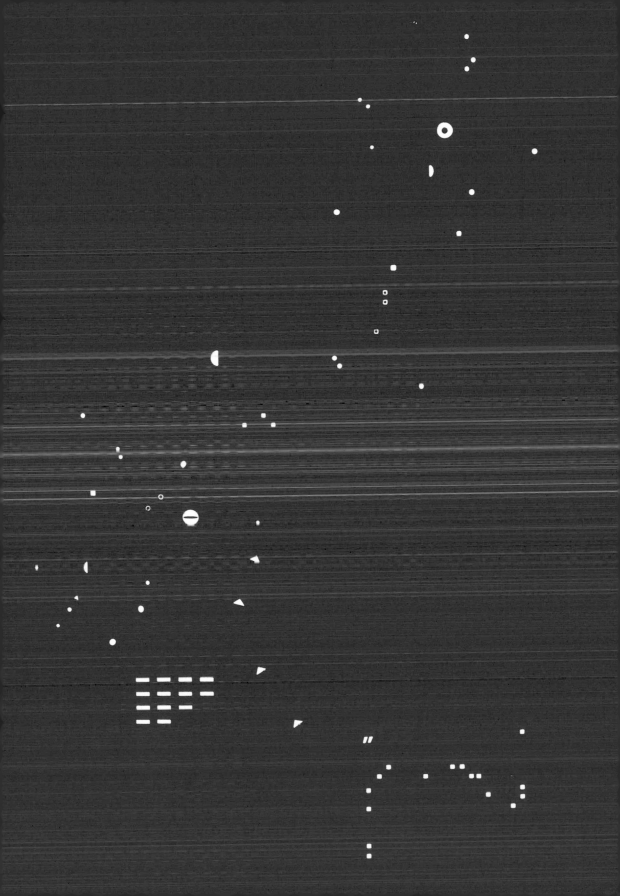

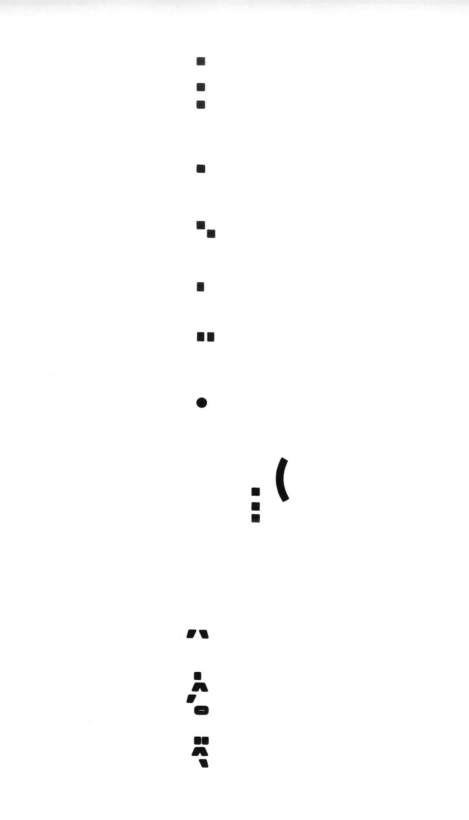

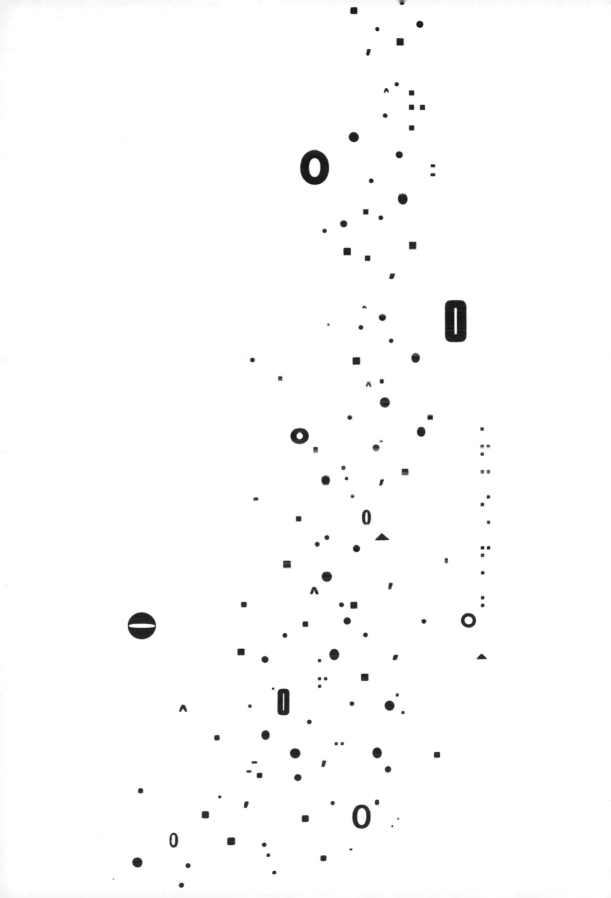

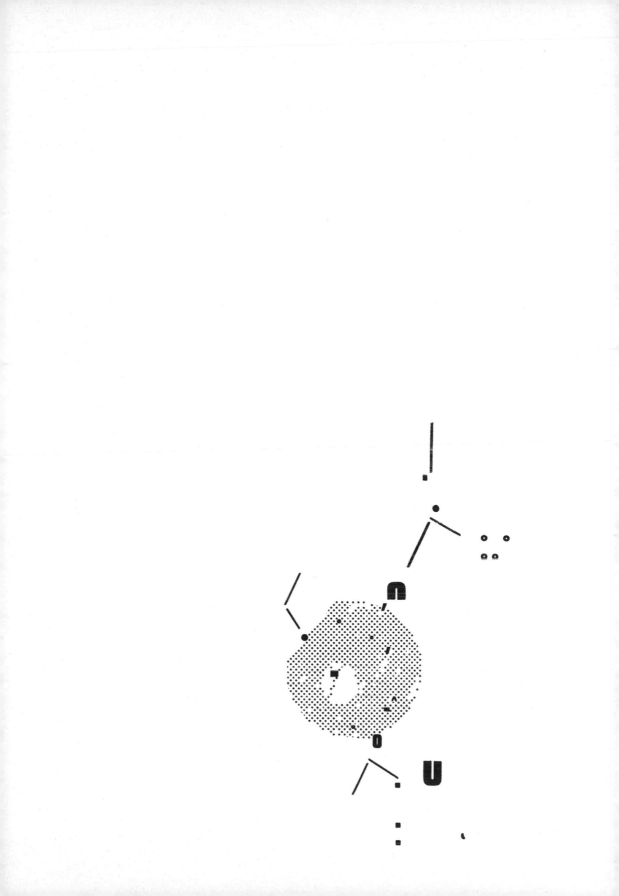

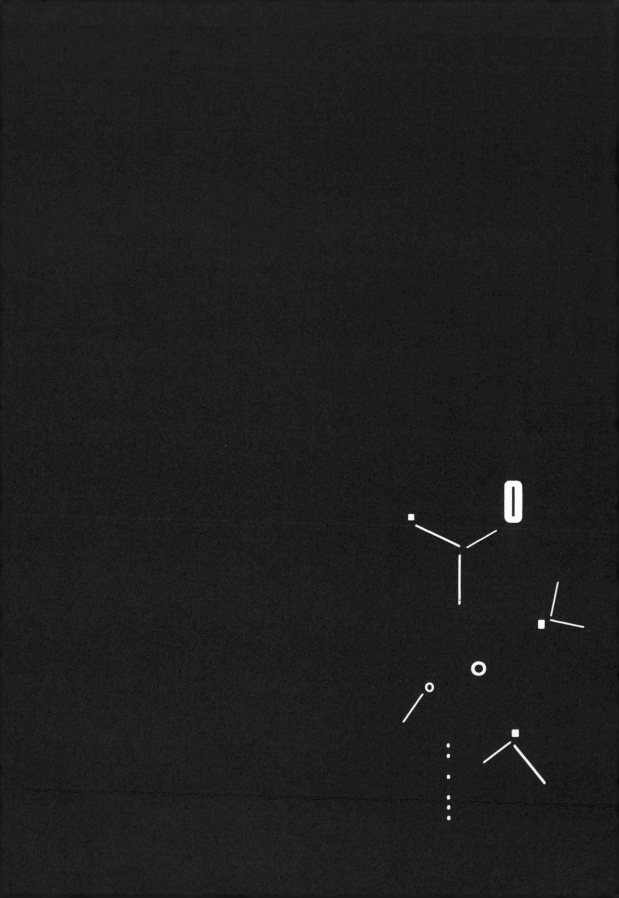

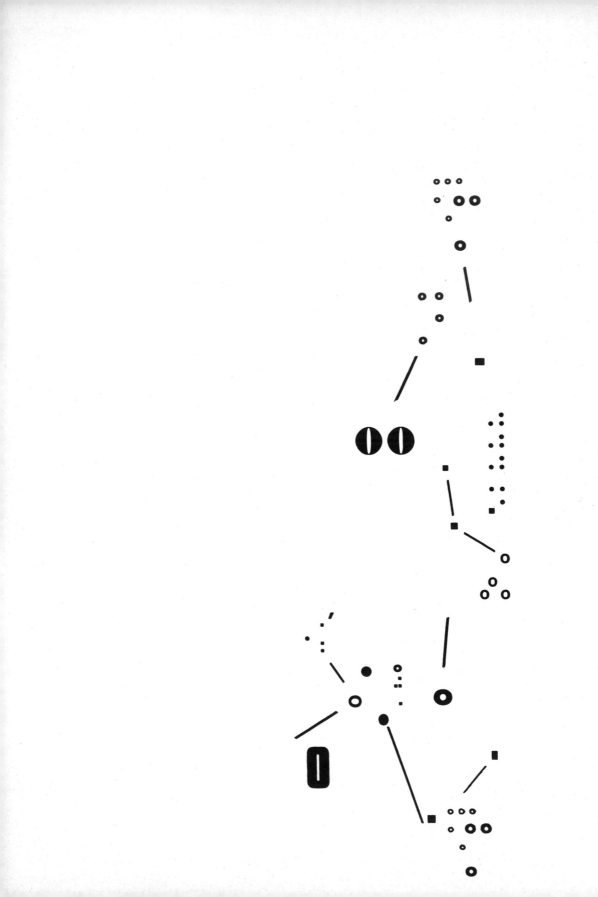

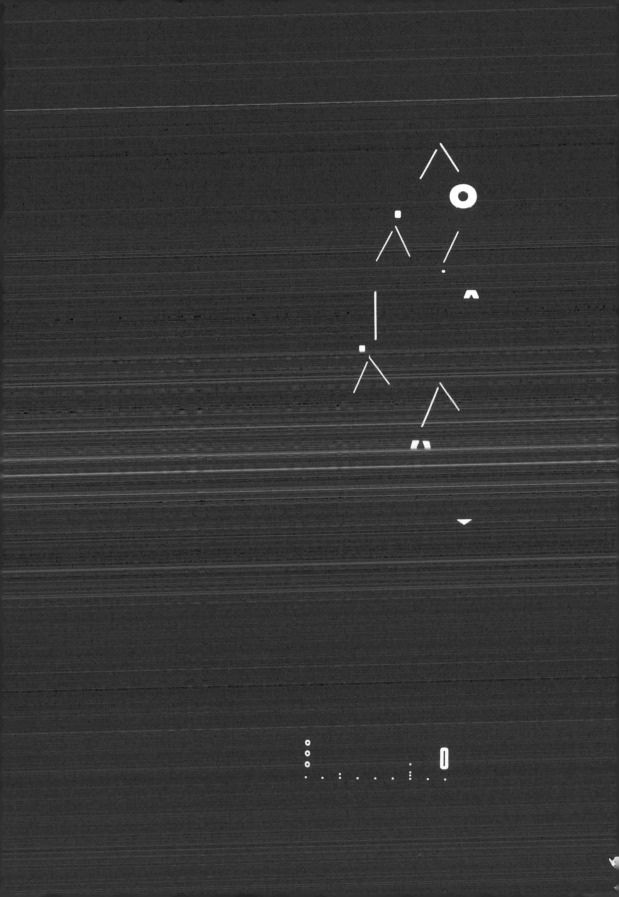

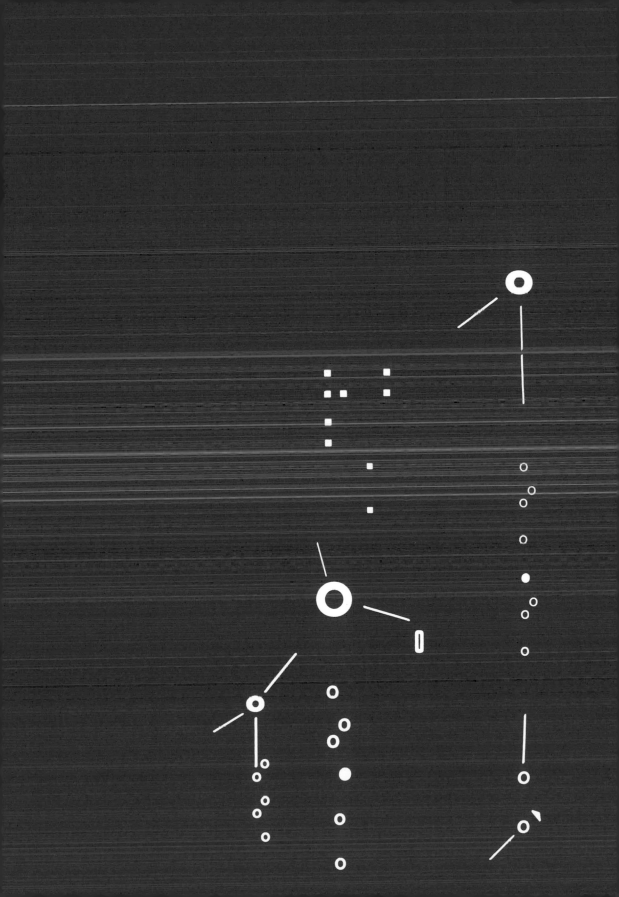

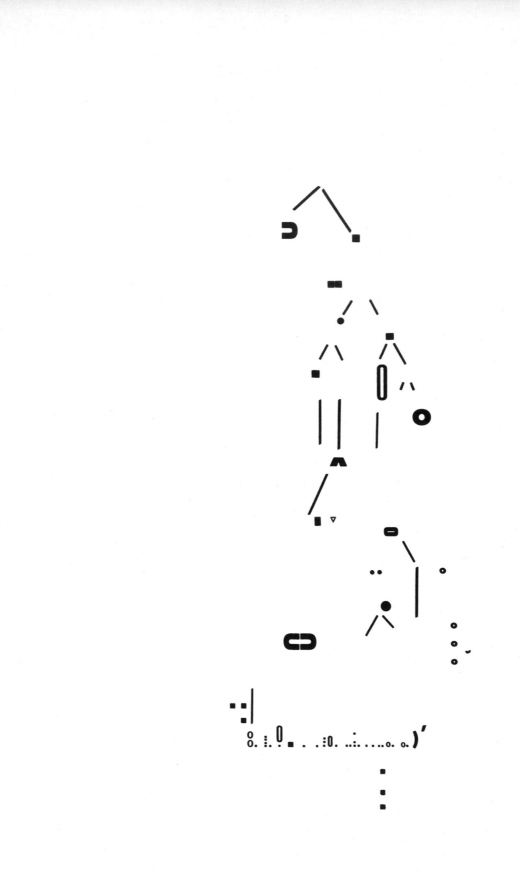

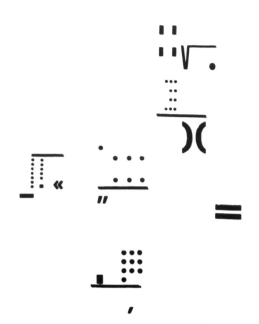

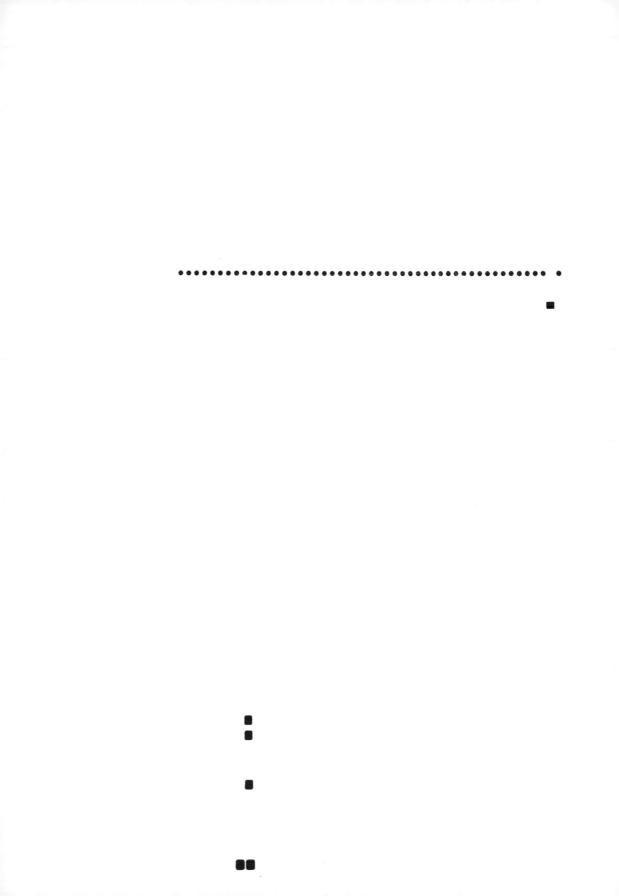

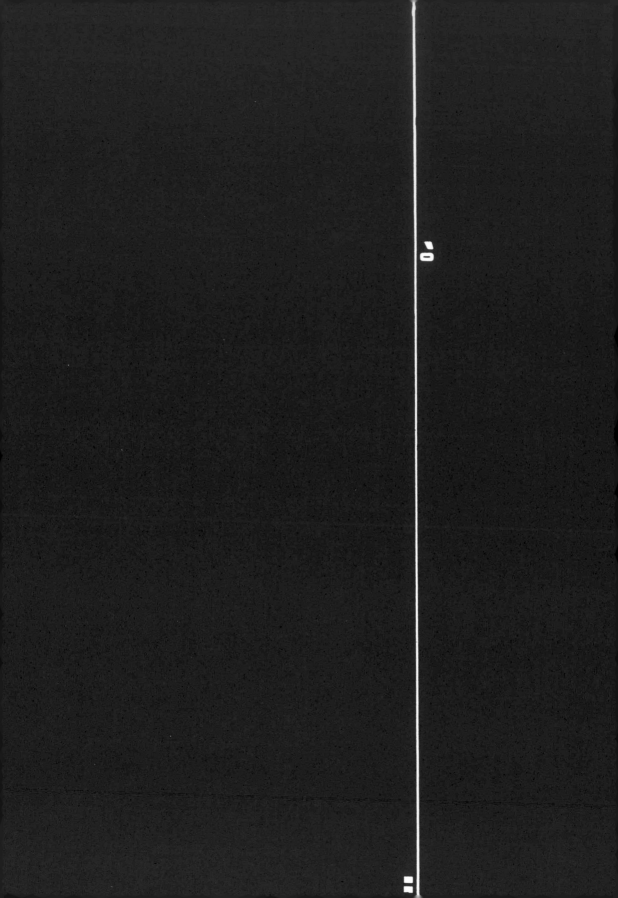

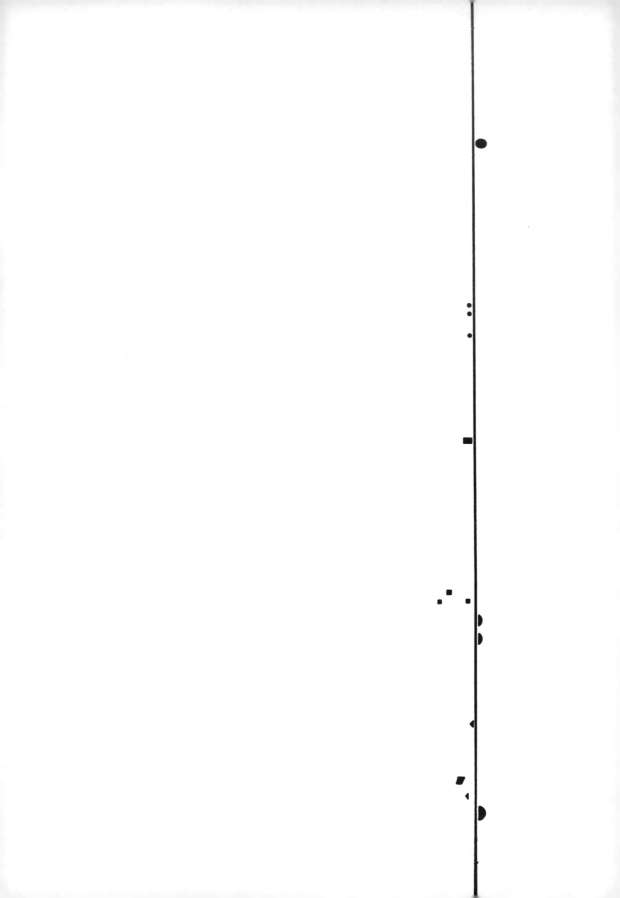

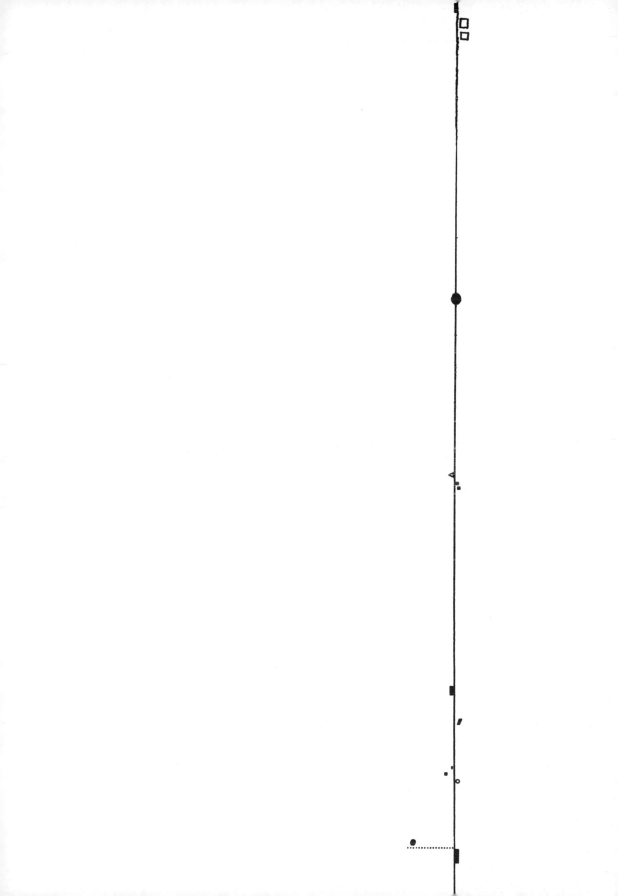

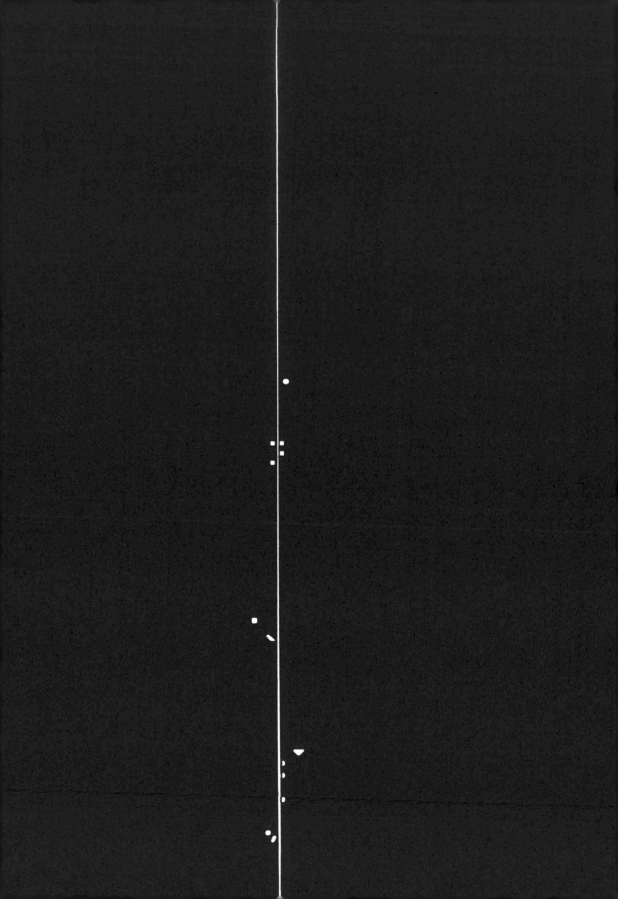

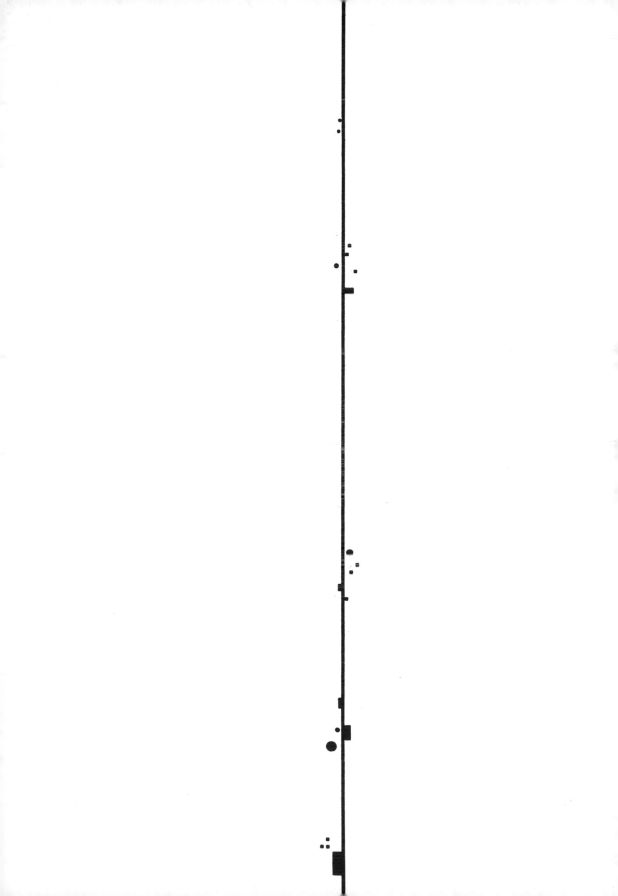

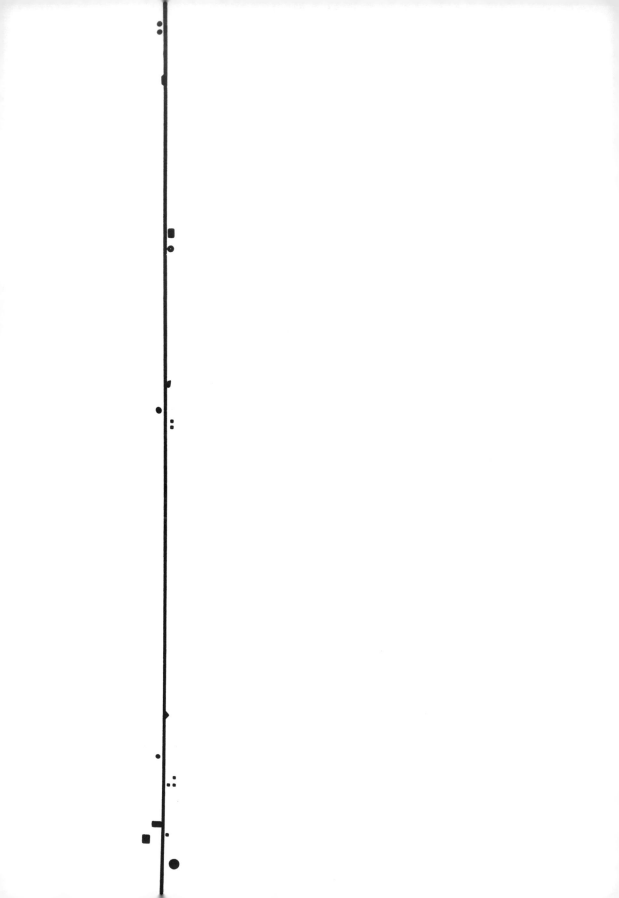

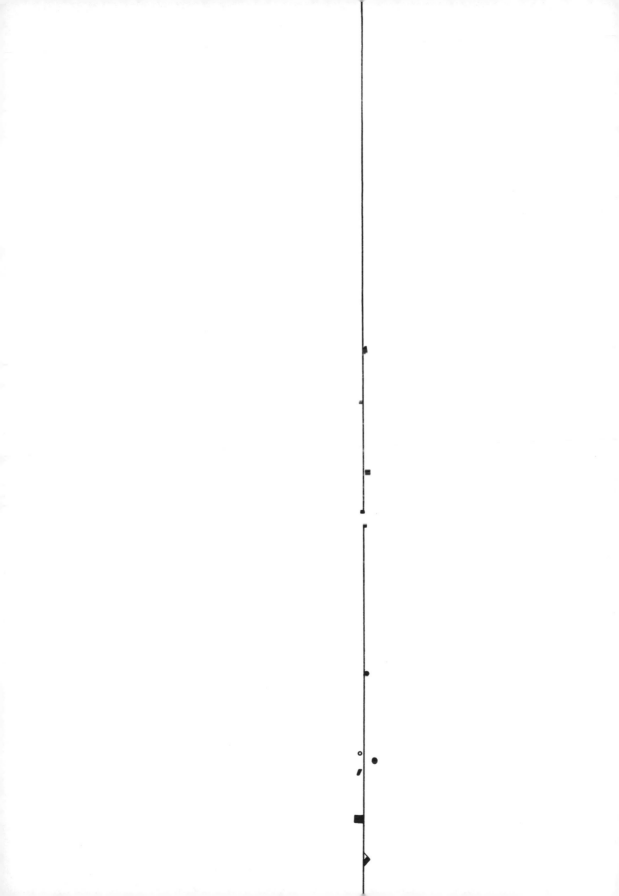

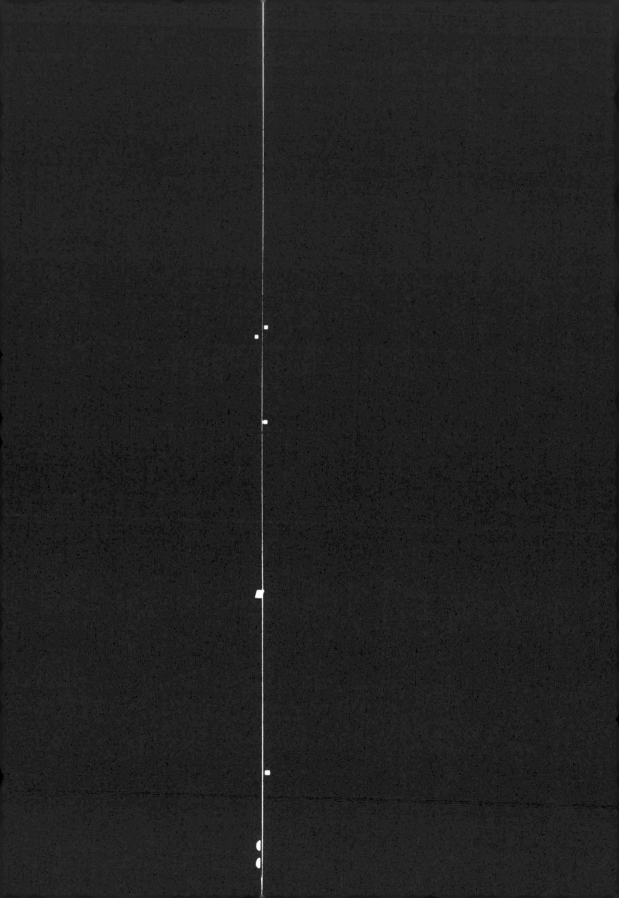

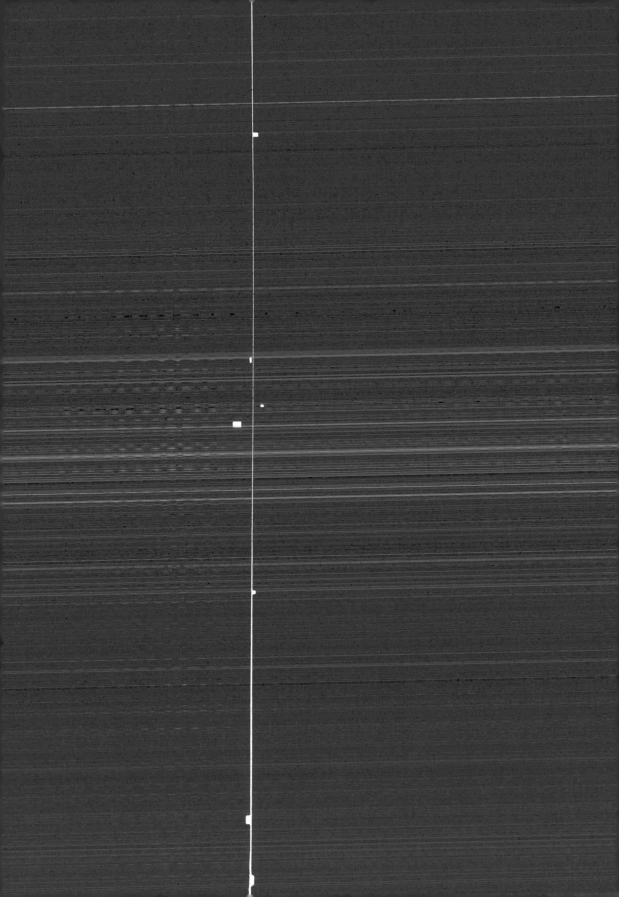

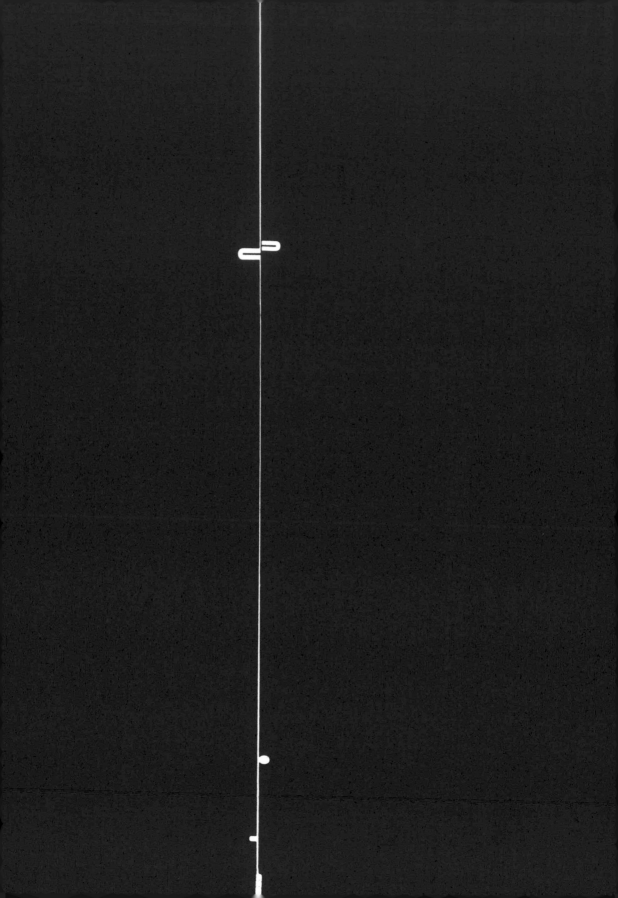

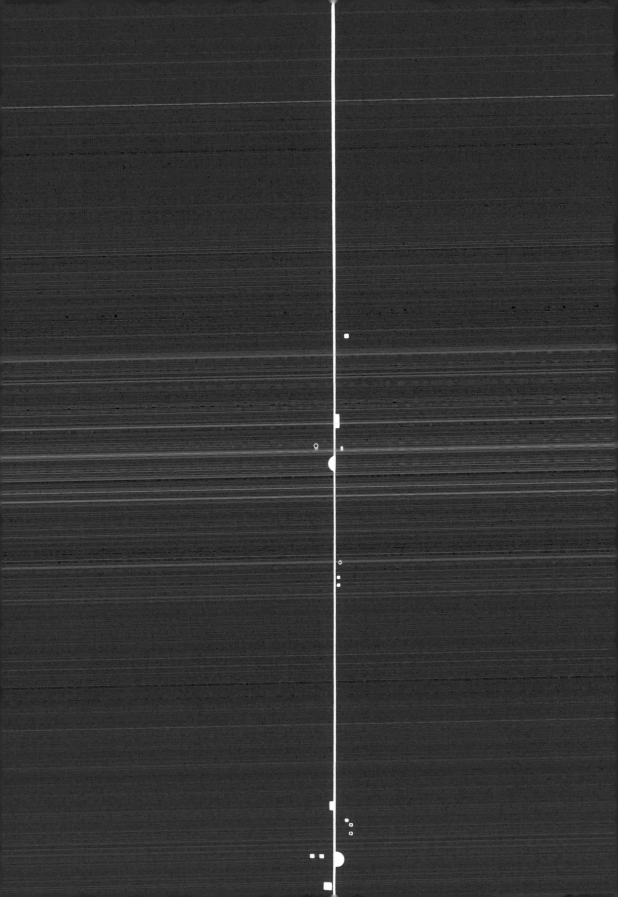

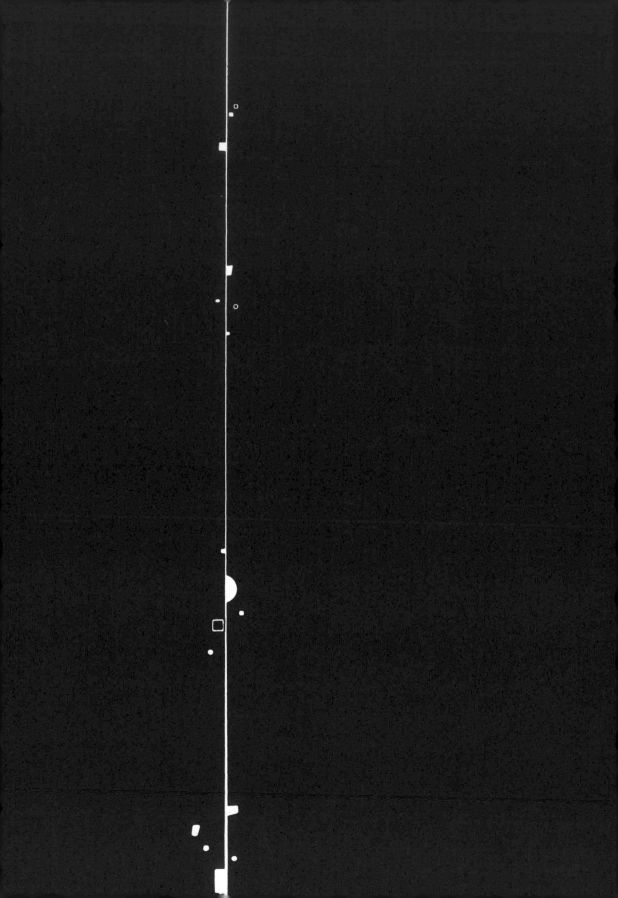

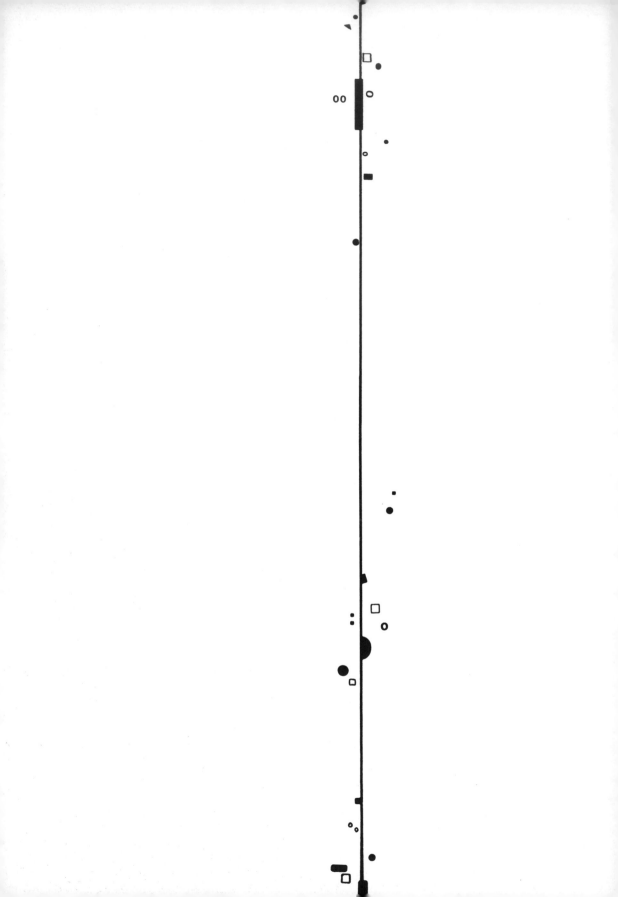

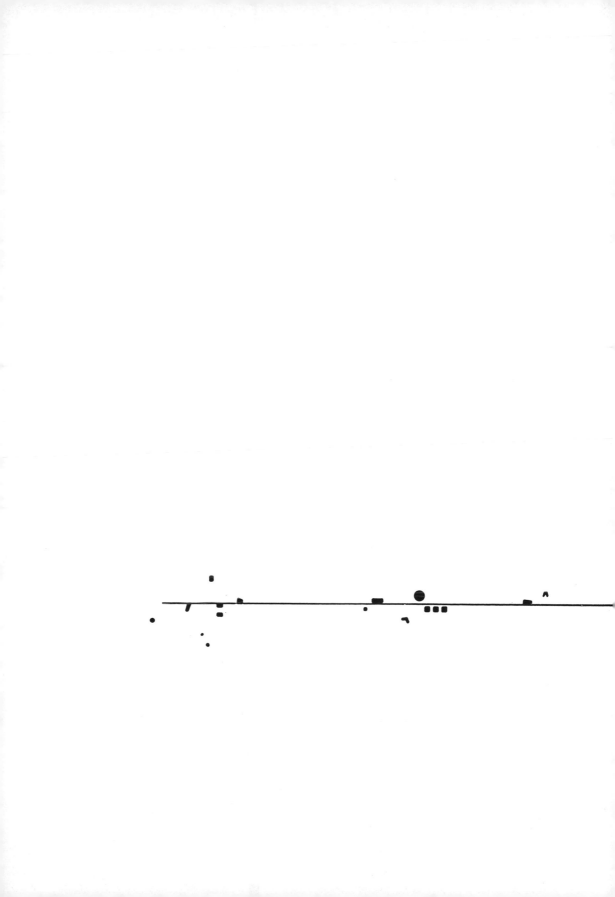

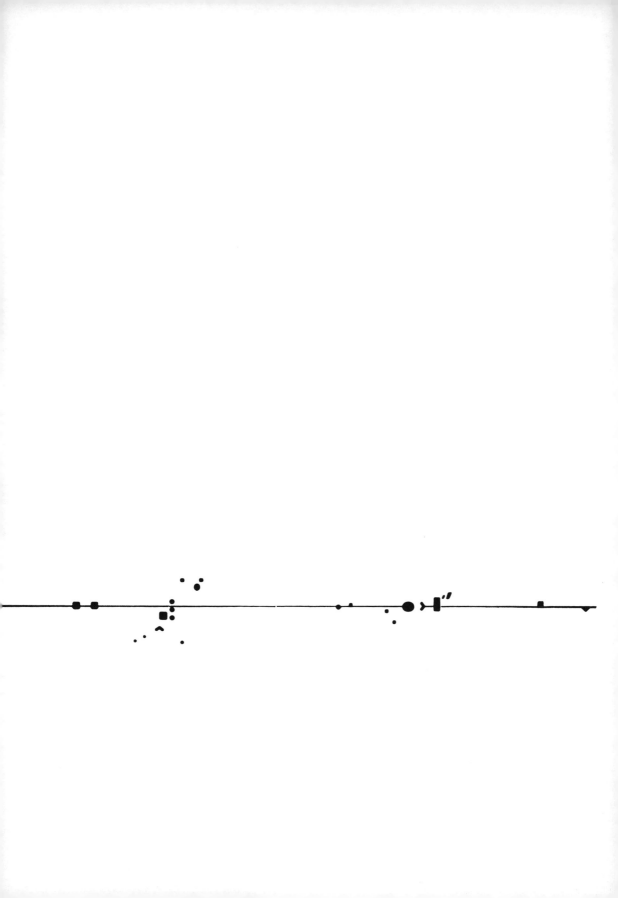

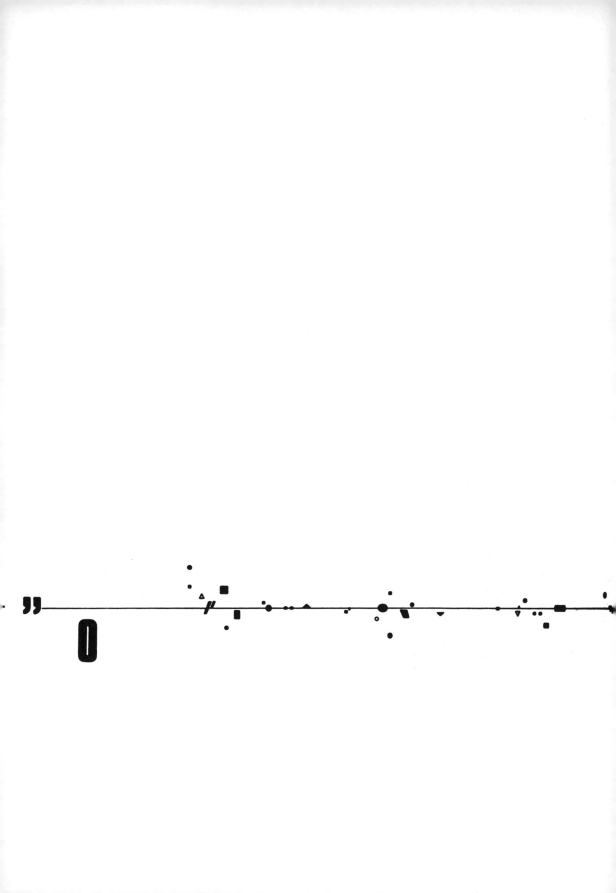

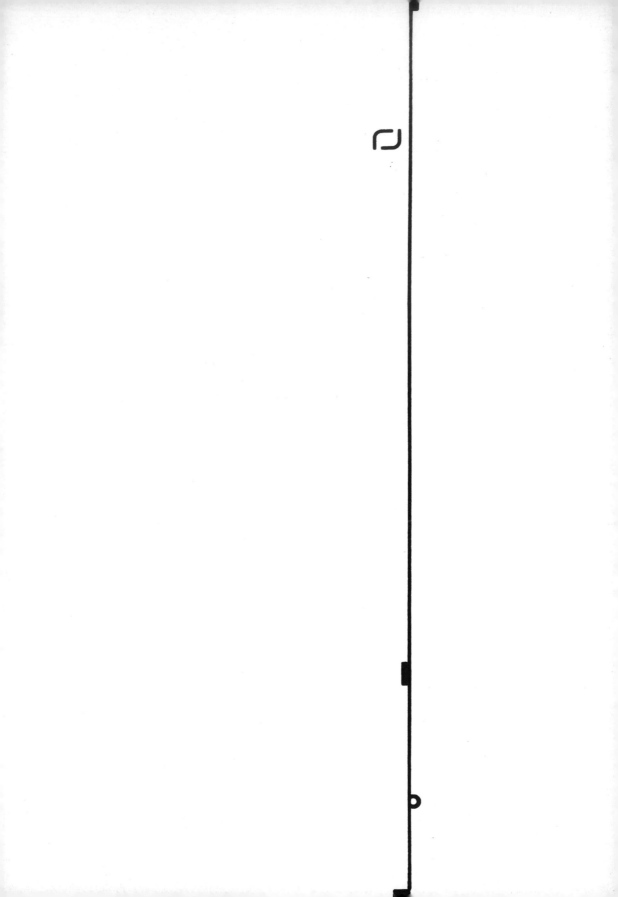

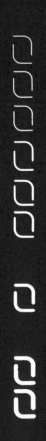

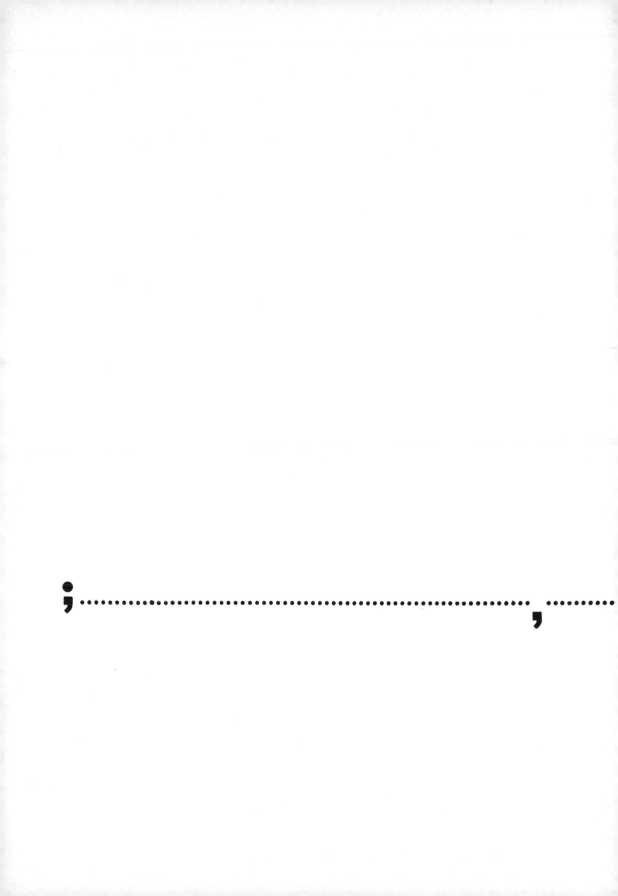

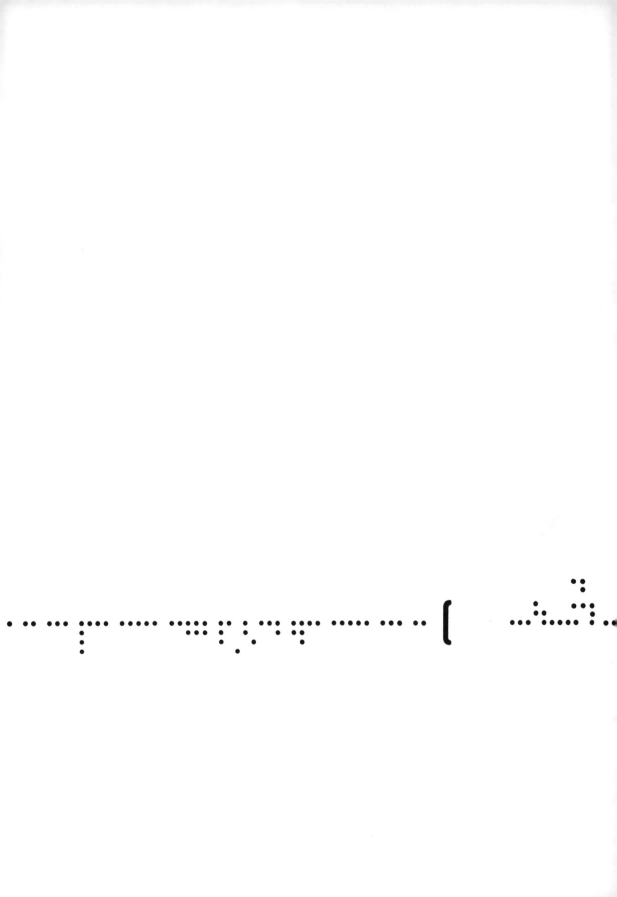

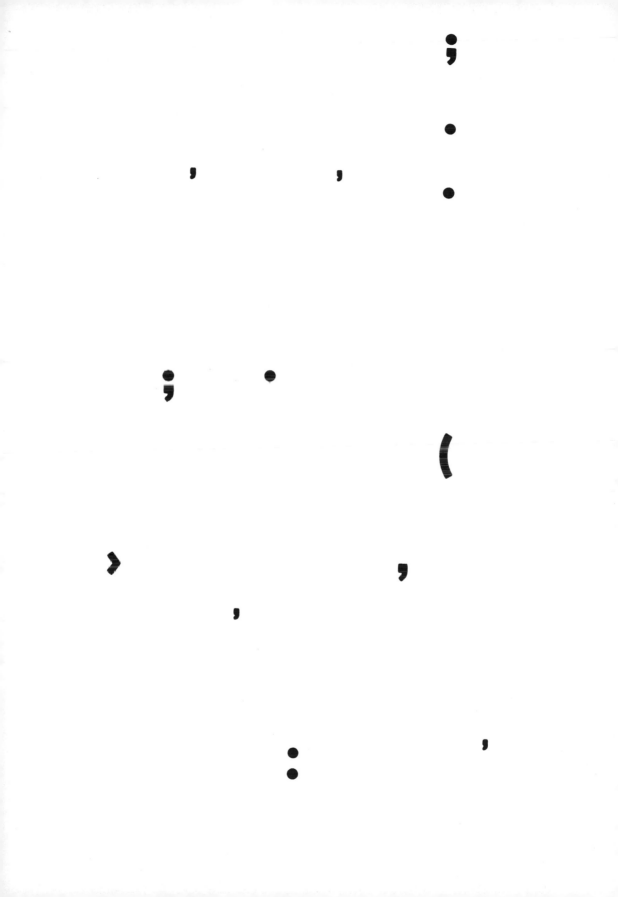

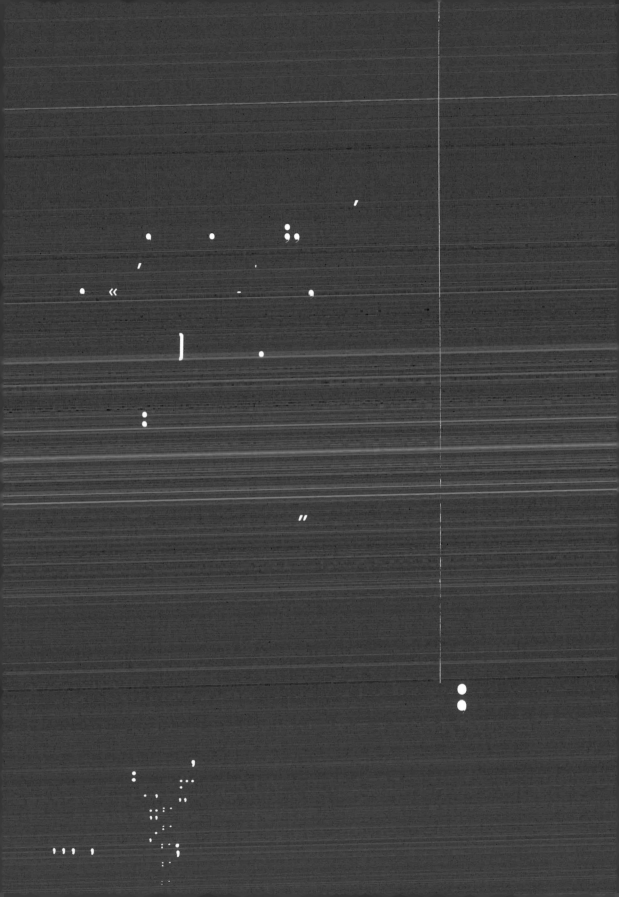

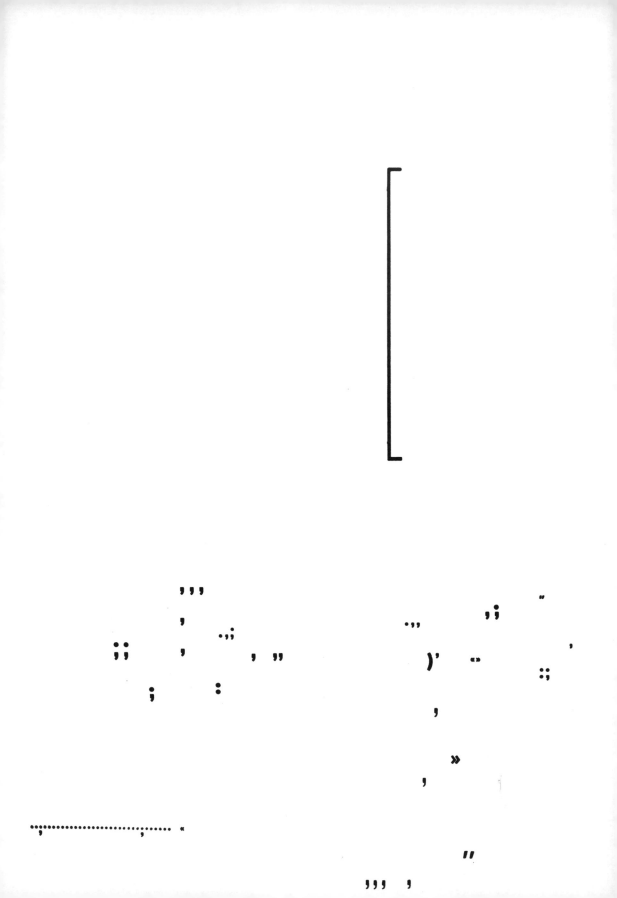

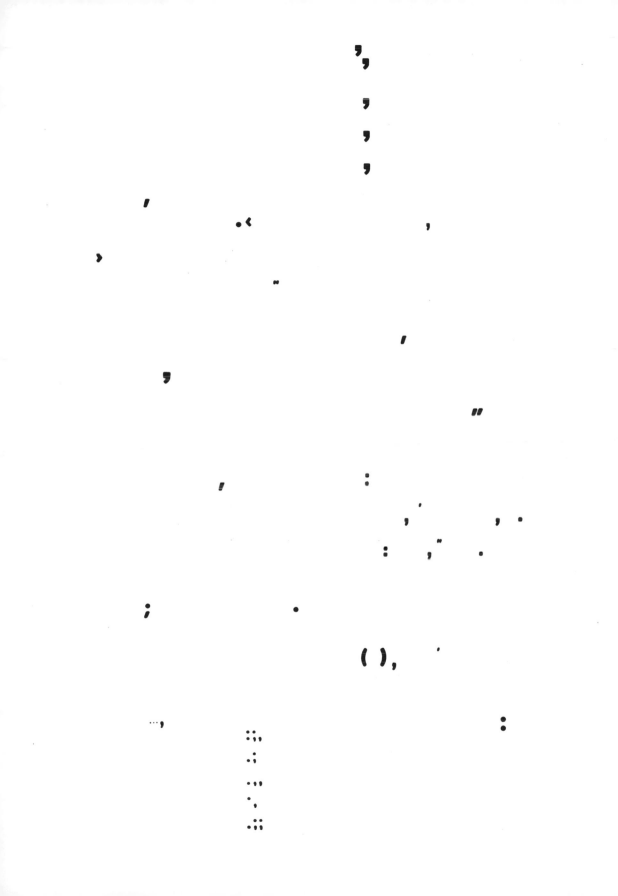

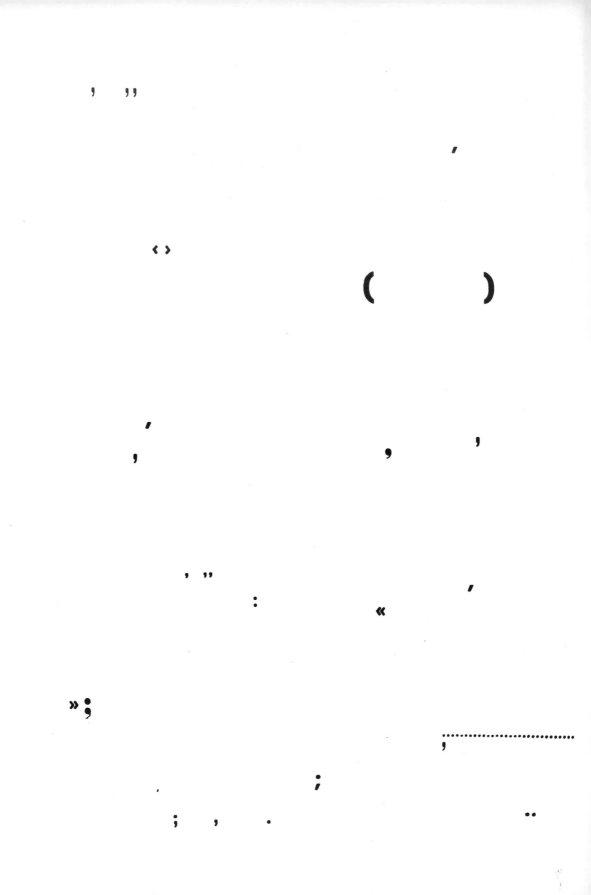

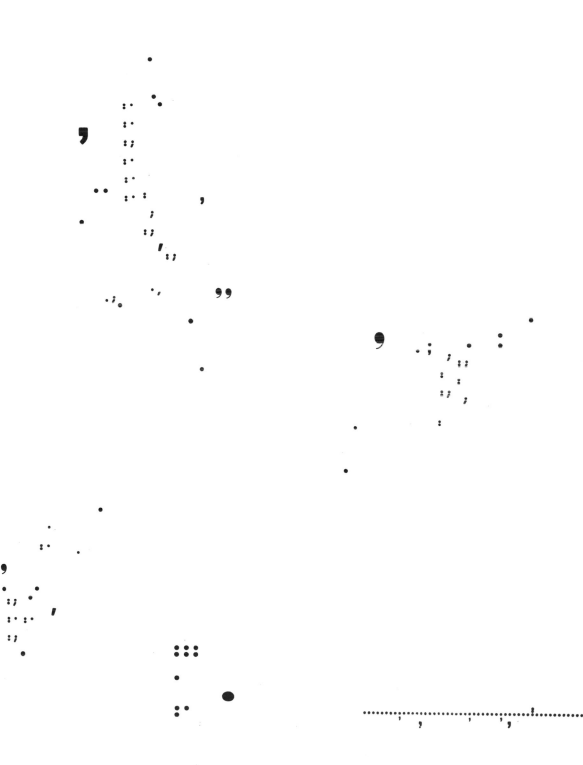

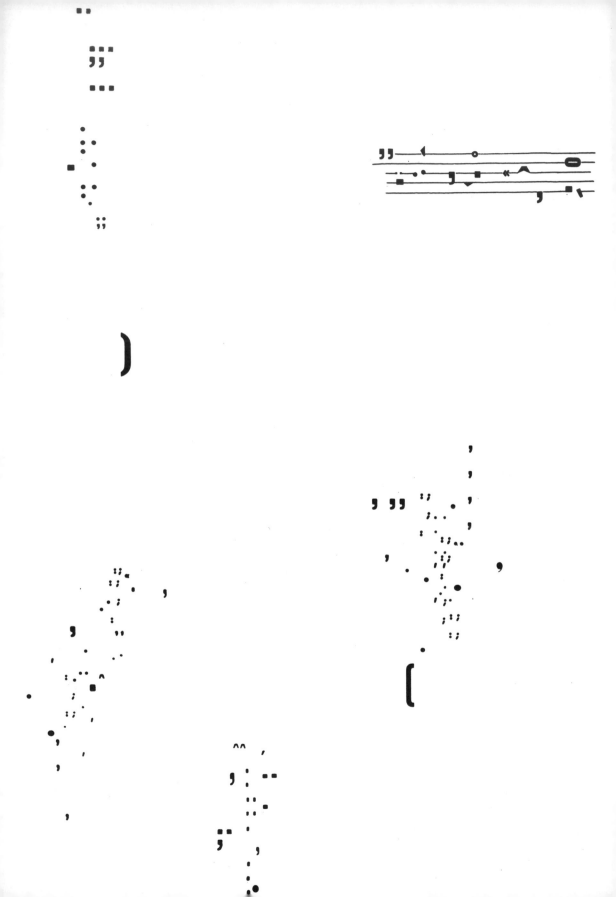

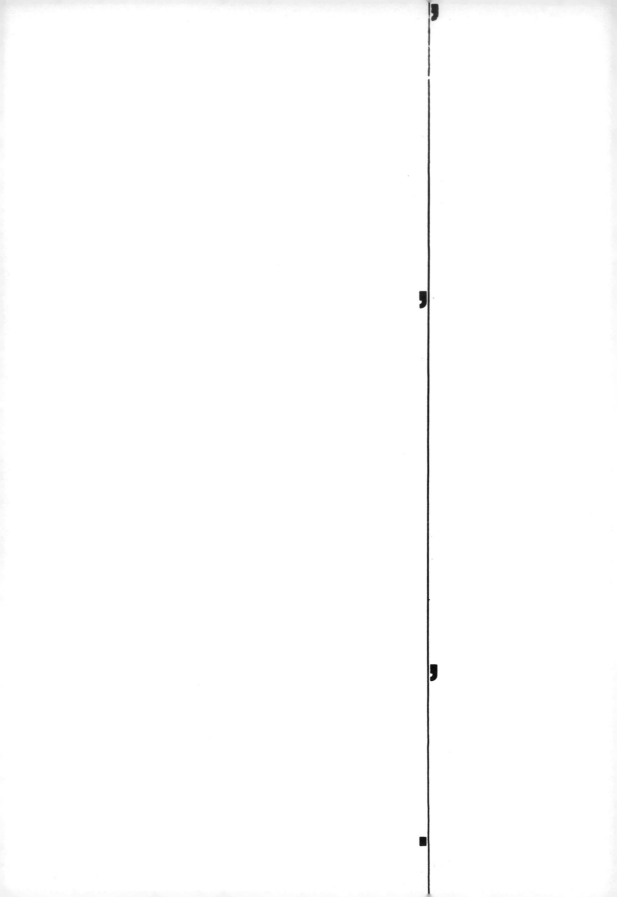

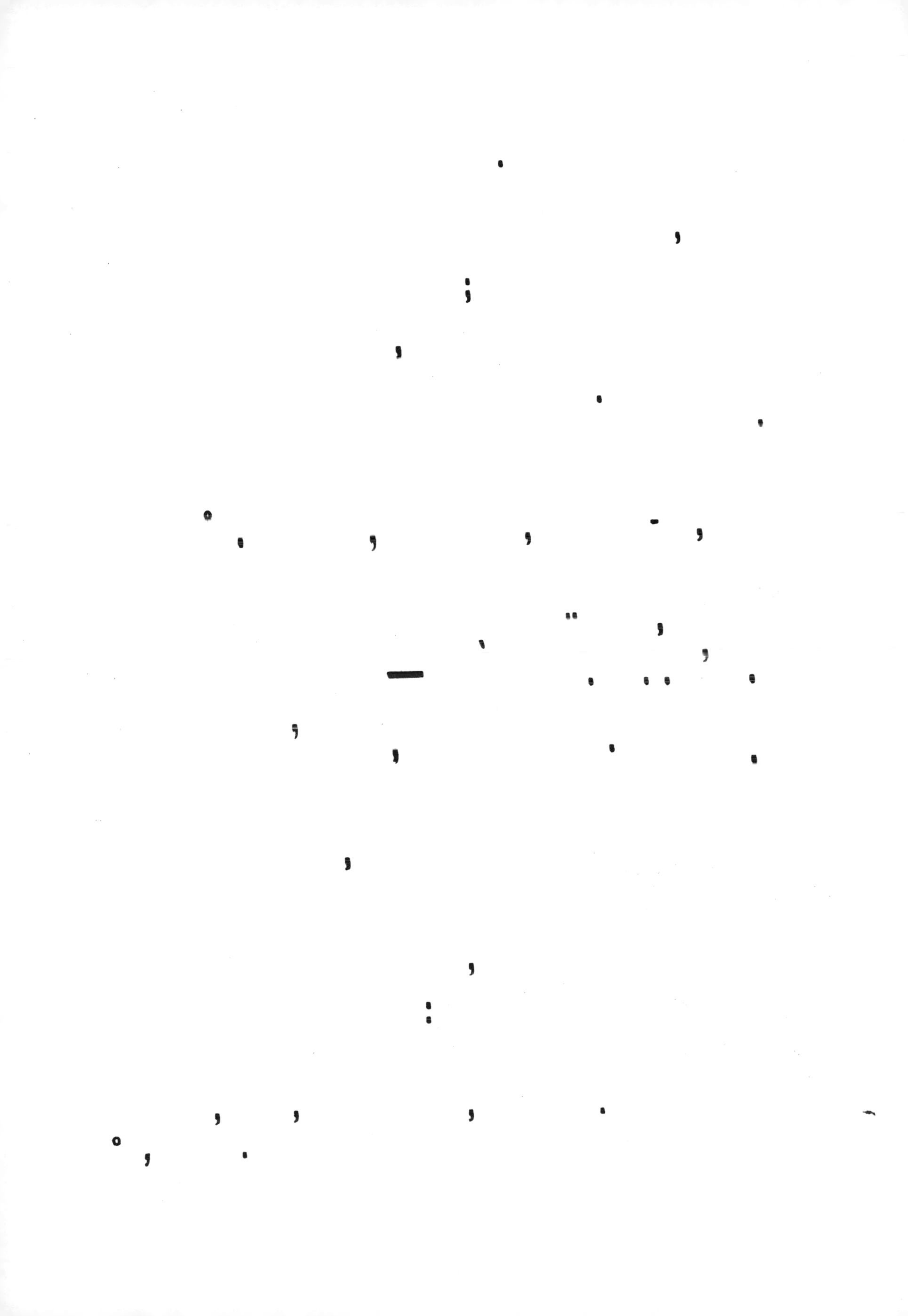

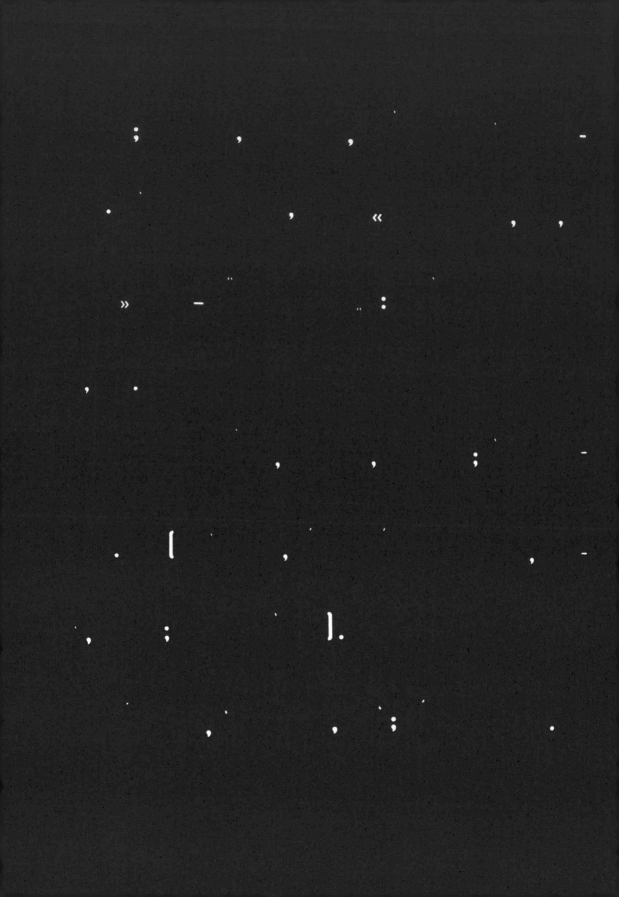

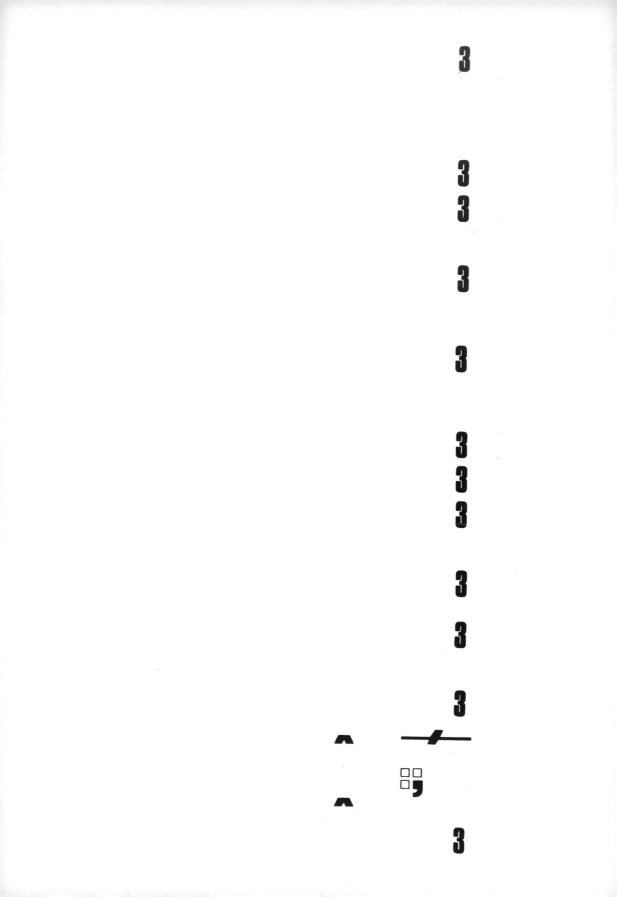

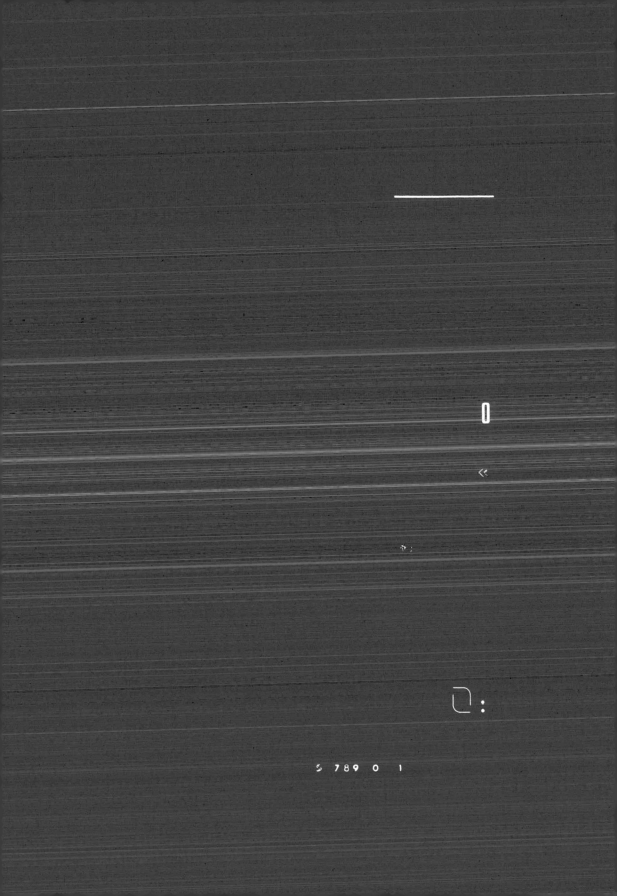

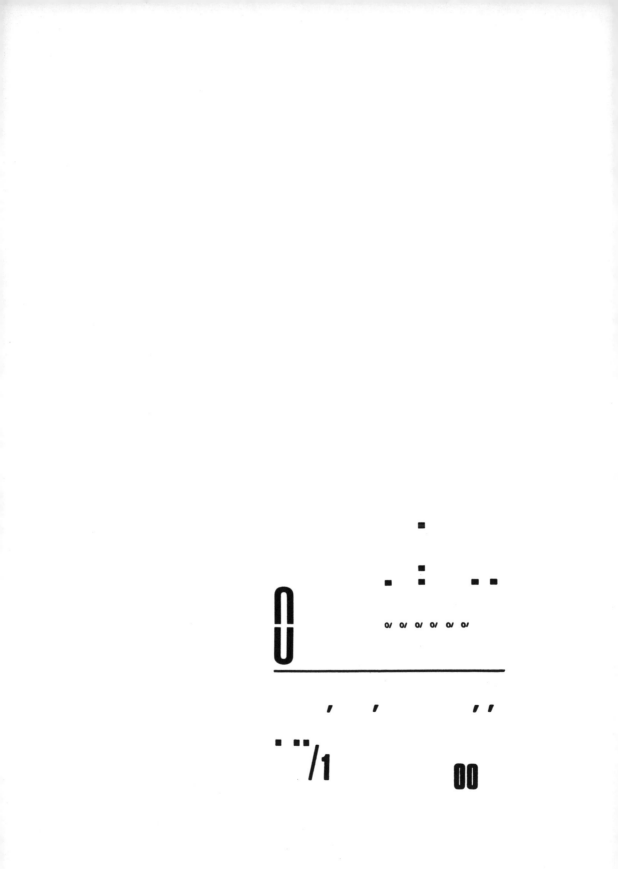

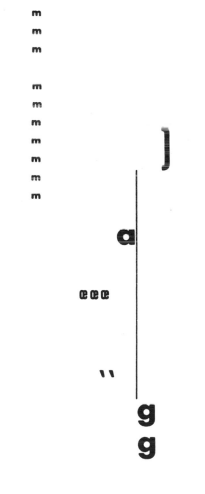

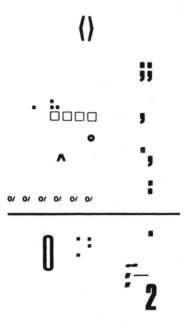

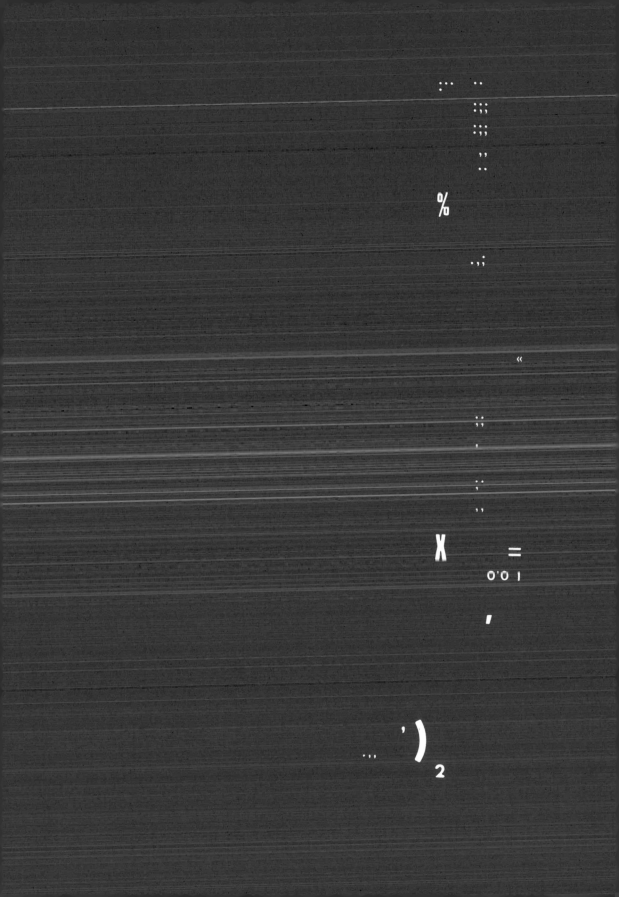

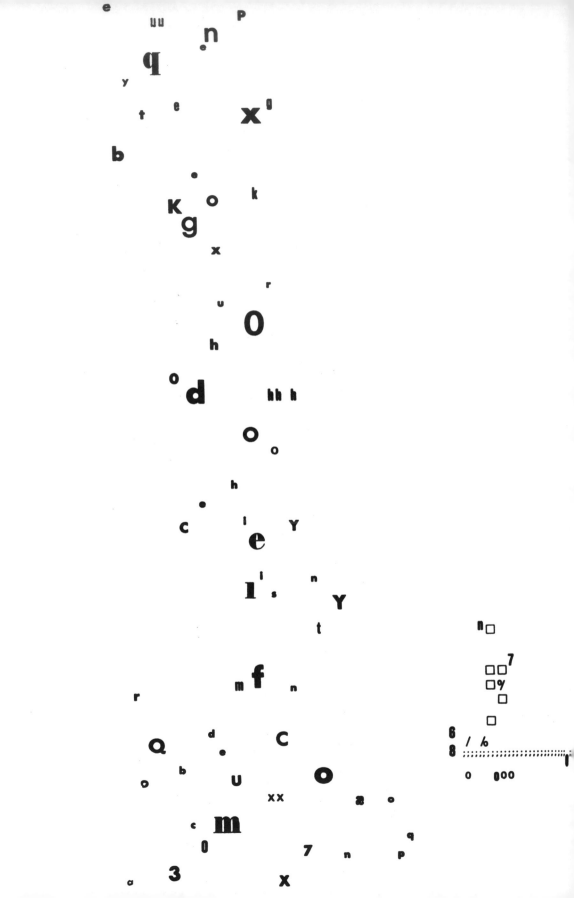

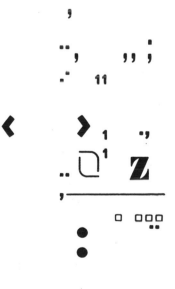

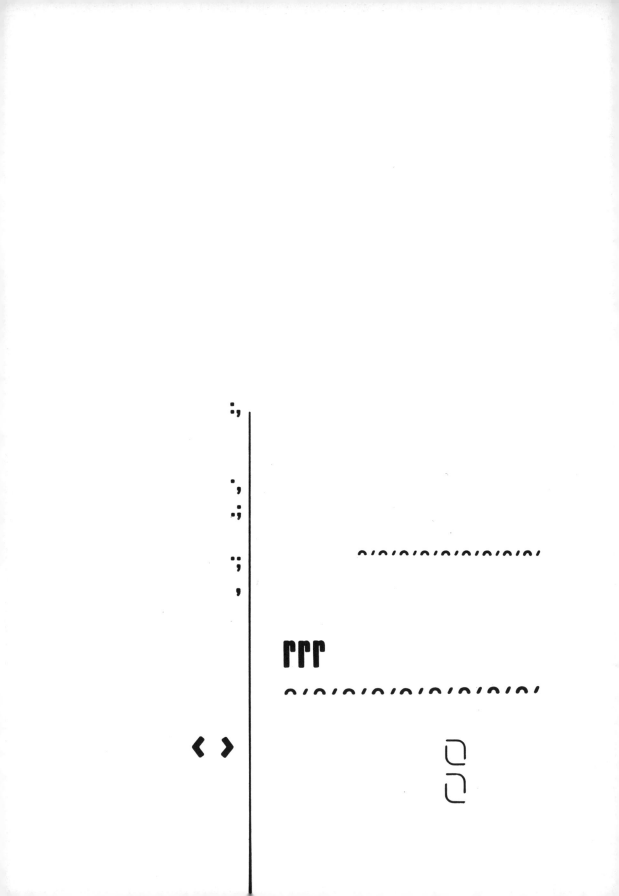

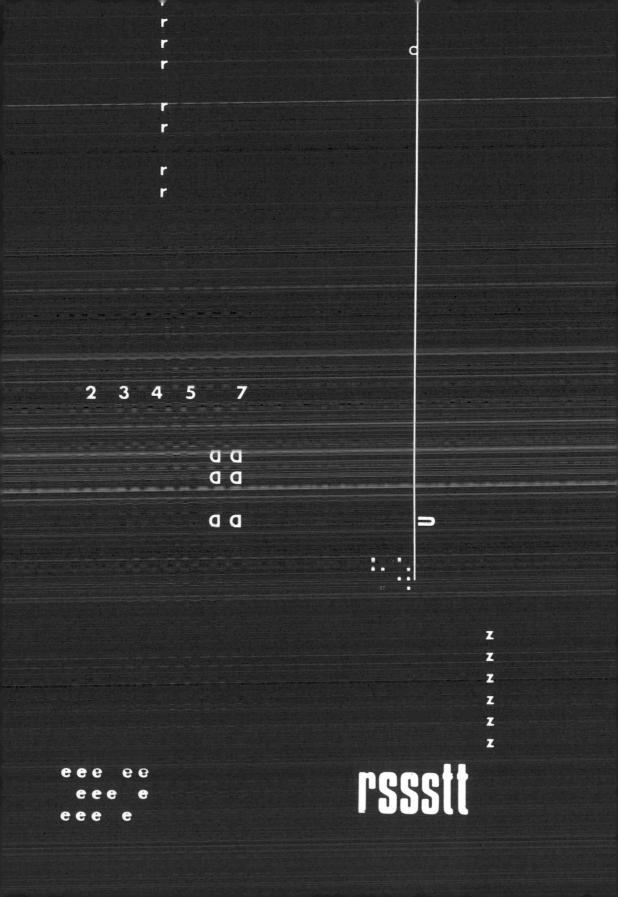

r
r
r
r
r
r
r
2 3 4 5 7
z
z
z
z
z
z
eee ee
eee e
eee e
rssstt

f
f
f

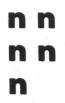
n n
n n
n

w x

e e e e

g

m
m

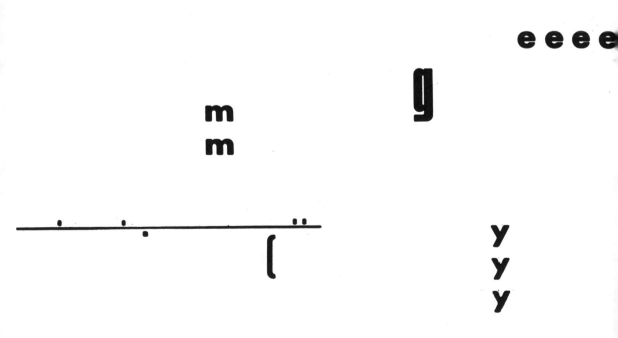

y
y
y

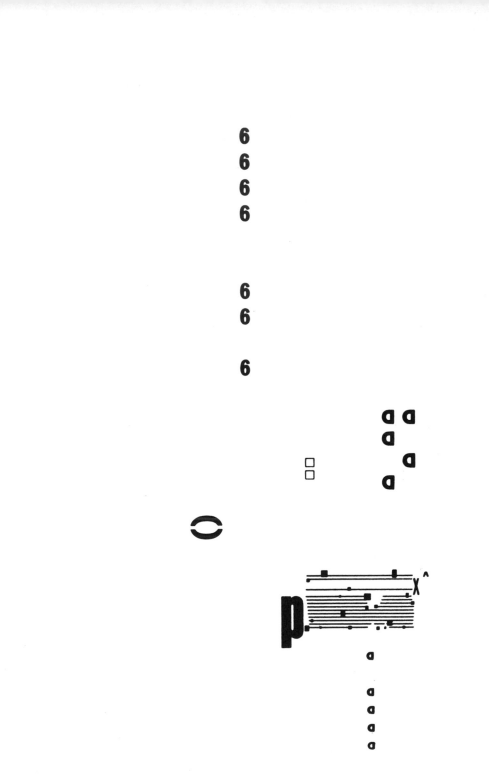

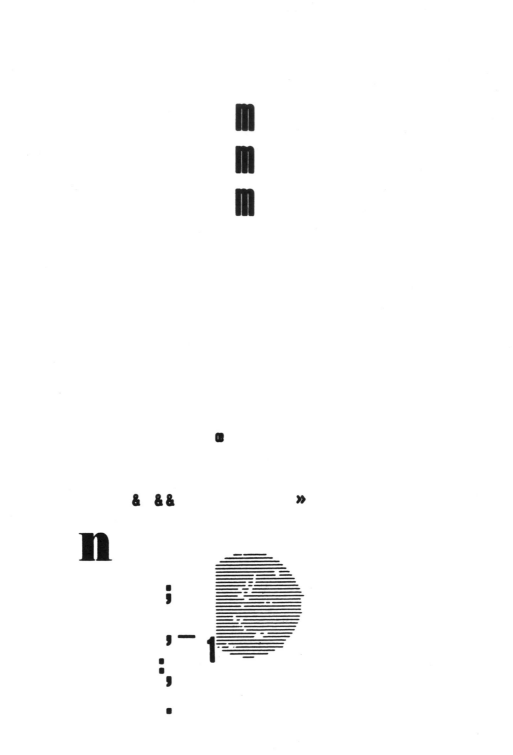

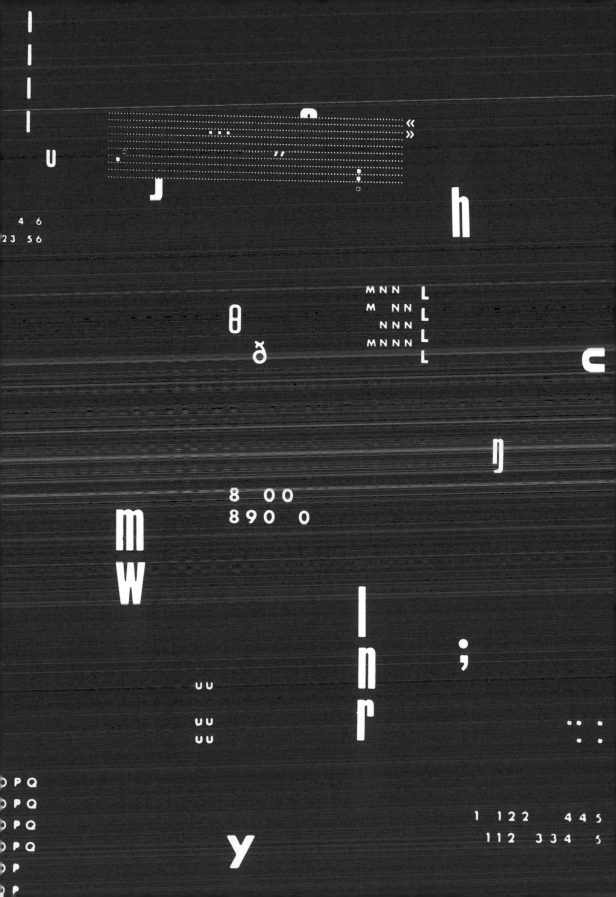

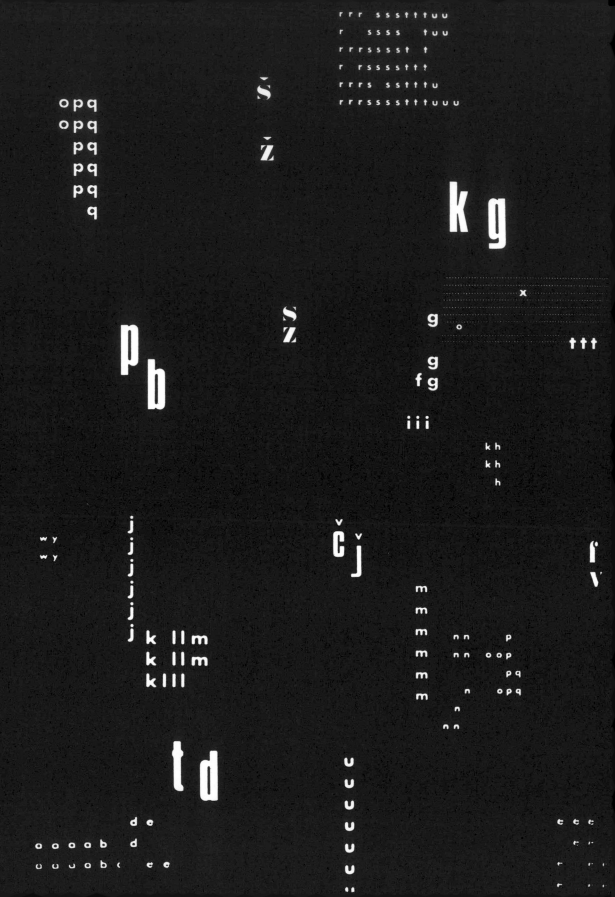

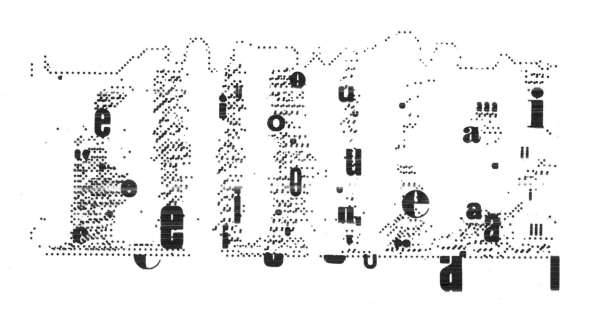

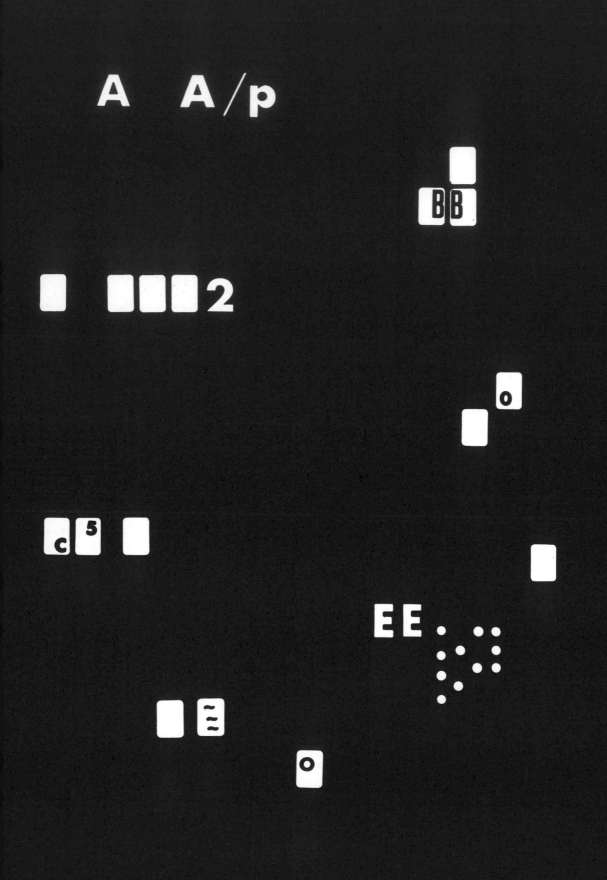

aaabbccddeeeef ghhi jk llmmn

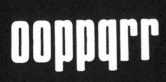

rss ttt uuvvw xyyz

zzaabb c eeeef ghhijklllm

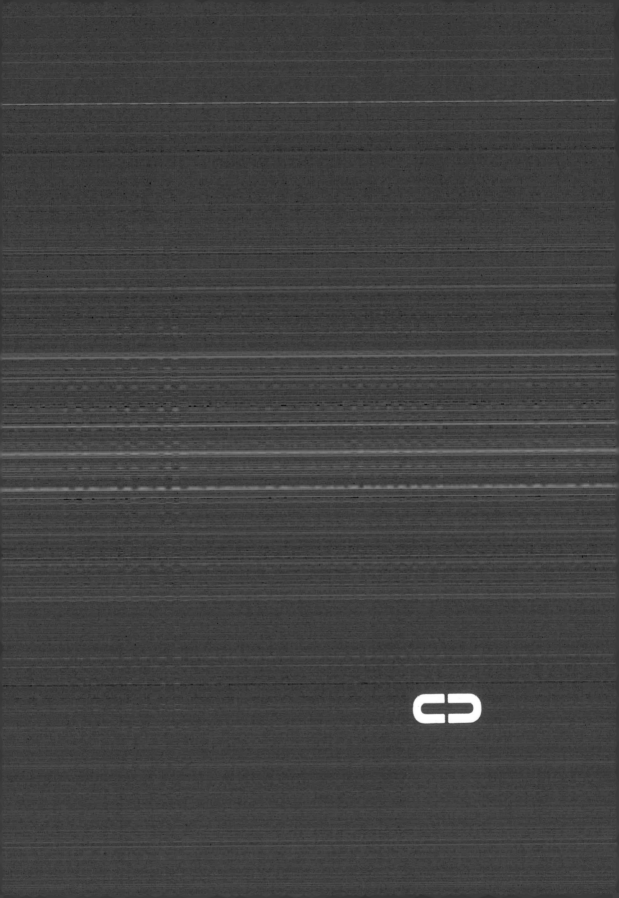

indice

capitolo zero
capitolo tre

point counter space

sincronic
diacronic   romance

avventura dentro il segno

segno/arti visive = metalinguaggio visivo

ricerca protostrutturologica /appunti per /ricerca
        delle costanti universali della semiotica

criptoritmi/visual concerto

coats of arms/itinerari/mappe

più uno

sentimental journey through

graphemes / phonemes / morphemes / tagmemes / sememes
allographs   allophones allomorphs   allosems

processi primari

ridondanza/emittente/ricevente

rapporti operativi/decodificazione aperta

there are more things Horatio

signum est res

but a new invention /as Alice said to herself

                                        verificare per ex
            plus
8 citazioni da The Spectator
            saggi di linguistica strutturale
            Joyce (descrizioni, monologo interiore)
        e da Dylan Thomas

index

chapter zero
chapter three

point counter space

synchronic
diachronic   romance

adventure within the sign

sign/ visual arts = figurative metalanguage

protostructuralist research /notes for /research
        for the universal constants of semiotics

cryptorhythms/visual concerto

coats of arms/itineraries/maps

plus one

sentimental journey through

graphomes / phonemes / morphemes / tagmemes / sememes
allographs   allophones allomorphs   allosems

primary processes

redundancy/sender/receiver

operational relationships/open decoding

there are more things Horatio

signum est res

but a new invention /as Alice said to herself

                              to verify for ex

        plus

8 quotes from The Spectator
                essays on structural linguistics
                Joyce (descriptions, interior monologue)
        and from Dylan Thomas

Giovanna Sandri
Capitolo Zero

Originally published in 1969
as #3 in the Marcalibri series
by Lerici in Rome

This edition designed by
Alec Mapes-Frances,
based on the original edition

Translated from the Italian
by Glacomo Sartorelli

DABA
68 Washington Avenue
Brooklyn, NY 11205
dabapress.net

Distributed by
ARTBOOK | D.A.P.
75 Broad Street, Suite 630
New York, NY 10004
www.artbook.com

Printed by die Keure in Belgium
in an edition of 500

DABA 009
ISBN 978 1 7346817 8 9